Running in Place
INSIDE THE SENATE

James A. Miller

A TOUCHSTONE BOOK
Published by Simon & Schuster, Inc.
NEW YORK

Copyright © 1986 by James A. Miller

First Touchstone Edition, 1987

Published by Simon & Schuster, Inc.
Simon & Schuster Building
Rockefeller Center
1230 Avenue of the Americas
New York, New York 10020

TOUCHSTONE and colophon are registered trademarks
of Simon & Schuster, Inc.

Designed by Levavi & Levavi

Manufactured in the United States of America

1 3 5 7 9 10 8 6 4 2
1 3 5 7 9 10 8 6 4 2 Pbk.

Library of Congress Cataloging-in-Publication Data
Miller, James A. (James Andrew), DATE–
Running in place.

Includes index.
1. United States. Congresses. Senate. 2. United
States—Politics and government—1981–   . 3. Politics,
Practical. I. Title.
JK1161.M55   1986   328.73'071   85-27734
ISBN: 0-671-49928-9
ISBN: 0-671-63604-9 Pbk.

For Leatrice and Mark Miller
miei cari genitori

Acknowledgments

This project began at Oxford University where, from musty quarters crammed with clippings on American politics, the late Professor Philip Williams exhorted and challenged me. He is dearly missed.

At the Congressional Research Service, Daniel Mulhollan's enthusiasm and friendship were of tremendous value. At the Senate library, Jean Winslow proved tireless in her willingness to be of assistance. The Institute for Educational Affairs provided a generous grant. Alice Mayhew, Robert Asahina, and Tod Lindberg, my editors, expended fortitude and wisdom. Robert Ellis Miller offered sagacious support. I am also grateful to Senator Howard Baker and his entire staff for their fellowship, and to all those in the Senate who freely discussed with me their professions, beliefs, and folkways.

Finally, my deepest gratitude belongs to Thomas William Shales, whose unyielding faith and countenance enables me to feel like I have a brother after all.

Contents

We do not get to know people when they come to us; we must go to them to learn what they are like.

—JOHANN WOLFGANG VON GOETHE

Introduction

Once upon a time, on the thinly populated fringe of an unexplored continent, there was conceived a new nation. Its institutions were not stiff and chafing like boots but supple and comfortable like moccasins. The institutions were in the service of four million free persons, about 80 percent of whom lived within 20 miles of Atlantic tidewater.

The Constitution accommodated the swift and radical transformation of the little agricultural nation into a continental and industrial one. But by the late twentieth century some institutions were shells of their former selves. There had been no violent rupture. The institutions were continuous with those of the young Republic. But they were remarkably changed in function and self-understanding.

Arguably, the Senate is the most transformed of all the institutions designed by the Founders. The designing of it involved a subtle blending of political philosophies that less subtle persons considered (and still consider) incompatible. The Senate as it now functions involves a yawning gulf between original theory and contemporary practice. The only other institution that may have changed as substantially from the role the Founders envisioned is the Supreme Court. The answer to the question of whether the Court's nature and function has changed as much as the Senate's depends on a difficult judgment about the Founders' expectations: Did they envision the exercise of judicial review in anything like the modern manner? If they did, then the Senate certainly is the institution most transformed from the original conception.

According to the incomparable Aristotle, the best regime is a mixed regime—a mixture of aristocratic and democratic elements. The Senate was destined to be such a mixture. It was to be an aristocratic (and Aristotelian) leavening of the American Republic.

The structure of the Republic's central government, with its separation of powers and system of checks and balances, is itself a tempering of pure democracy. So is the republican principle, which is the principle of representation: In a republic, the people do not decide issues, the people decide who shall decide. The Senate was supposed to be somewhat insulated from the normal tumults of popular government. It was not to be an exception to the principle of popular government but was to involve the practice of popular government by, shall we say, indirection.

The thirty-year-age threshold for membership, the six-year term, and the method of election by state legislatures (abandoned in 1913) were supposed to make the Senate a more deliberative body than the House of Representatives, which was supposed to be markedly more plebiscitary. The equal representation of the states violates the democratic principle, especially as that principle is currently understood (by the Supreme Court and other simplifiers) in the slogan about "one man, one vote." A senator was supposed to enjoy enough independence to enable him to be an educator of his constituents.

In the exquisite word of the founding era, democracy was to be "mitigated." The Senate was to be a mitigation. It could not mitigate if it did not depart, however, delicately, from purely democratic values. Its attributes were to teach a truth that needs and deserves reiteration: equality is not a synonym for justice.

The weakening of the discipline and structure of American

political parties has coincided with, and to some extent has been hastened by, the revolutions in political fundraising and communication. This, and the brokering ethic of interest-group liberalism, has contributed to the weakening leadership within the Congress. All this has produced within Congress an ethos of severe individualism. Senators and congressmen have become political entrepreneurs, measuring their political health, and having their effectiveness measured, in terms of the personal publicity they receive.

It was an event of symbolic importance when the House and Senate built for themselves television studios on the second floor of the Capitol. The studios were not strictly necessary. Members could step outside to the cameras on the lawn. But the studios did make vivid the extent to which senators, especially—the Senate having become the breeding ground of presidential candidates—comprise a lonely crowd of restless, nervous and often exhausted people in pursuit of ephemeral satisfactions. Today's senators complain that the body has a weak institutional sense and a declining institutional memory. But it does offer visibility to individuals.

Gladstone served in the House of Commons for 60 years. He was a powerful and indefatigable public speaker in an era when political oratory was an important form of entertainment. In 60 years Gladstone's face and voice were seen and heard by fewer than those that see and hear a senator who manages to land a 20-second "sound bite" on one of the three network newscasts.

James Buckley was a senator from New York for one term, from 1971 to 1977. Looking back, with a civilized mixture of regret and relief, Buckley said that the workload of the Senate had doubled in his six years. Whether it has doubled again in the decade since then is a quantitative measurement that is difficult to make. That the quality of a senator's life is declining is a judgment in which most senators concur.

If the central government is going to be omnipresent and omniprovident, if it is going to try to fine-tune the equity of a complex continental society, using the direct provision of goods and services, subsidies and other incentives, and regulations, then there is going to be rapid growth in the size of the federal establishment. And there will be proportionate growth in the opportunities, meaning the temptations, for Congress to act.

There are only 50 states, and there are not apt to be any more soon. There are only two senators for each state: the Constitution is strict about this. This means that as the workload increases, the senators are increasingly dependent on staff. And that means that the staff is increasingly independent of close supervision by their harried senators. Thus, as the size of the staff grows arithmetically, the mischievousness grows exponentially.

Bryce Harlow served on the staffs of General George Marshall and Rep. Carl Vinson of the House armed services committee. Then he worked for Presidents Eisenhower, Nixon and Ford, trying with mixed success to tutor them in the fine art of peaceful coexistence with Congress. After four decades of closely observing Congress he concluded that most of its deficiencies are inherent in democracy and hence should not really be denounced. Most, but not all. He has seen so much folly; he is a hard man to alarm, but he is alarmed by the growth of congressional staffs.

When he signed on with Rep. Vinson, Major Leslie Groves, who had directed the Manhattan Project, told him: "You are about to become a terrible danger to national security." Harlow asked why, and Groves replied: Because you are about to influence events, to cause battalions to move and policy to change, "and you really don't know a damn thing." Harlow recently told this story to Suzanne Garment of *The Wall Street Journal* (August 9, 1985), and added: "There are all those bright kids up there with essentially nothing to do—so they do deviltry. The Hill has become a very grave impediment to decent government, especially since Watergate gave them the idea they could administer the executive branch."

Once upon a time the Senate was described as the saucer

into which legislation was poured to cool. Readers of this volume can concoct their own metaphors for the modern Senate. They are not apt to think of it as a tranquil lagoon in a stormy world. It is more like a cork bobbing in the middle of the white-water river of American politics. Alexander Hamilton proposed a permanent Senate, with members serving during good behavior. There are several ways of thinking about that idea in the light cast by Jim Miller's account of the texture of life in today's Senate.

—George F. Will

Prologue

This is a book about two women, ninety-eight men, and thousands who attend them. It is also a story of how their experiences, expectations, frustrations, and personalities influence the quality and character of public service, of American life and even of world affairs.

To know these individuals is to know the modern Senate.

To know the modern Senate is to know a legislative body in the throes of traumatic change. In the past ten years, the Senate has grown into a gigantic conglomerate—out of touch with its subsidiaries and stockholders, and unable to meet even the challenge that its own board of directors sets for it. Bloated, overburdened, and increasingly polarized, its members increasingly finding themselves disillusioned and powerless, the Senate is drawing America toward a true legislative crisis—but few people know it.

I did not know it either when I came to my job in the Senate in 1981. As a political science major with a fair degree of knowledge and a lot of interest, I was aware of the formal structures in Congress, but I soon realized how little I knew about the crucial, informal structures. My impression was the still-popular one of the Grand Old Senate—an exclusive club that moved at a courtly pace set by a dominant group of respected, gray-haired elders, most of them southerners who had served in the Senate for the bulk of their natural and political lives, and who managed the Senate with a common ethos and attitude. Nothing had prepared me for understanding day-to-day existence in the modern Senate, or for how dramatically individuals shape this institution. That discovery led me to write this book.

It is my hope that a journey through the careers, corridors, offices, and hearing rooms of Capitol Hill will capture the realities of life inside an institution whose members seem ever more strong-minded, egotistical, and competitive; who exhibit less and less a willingness to submit to rules and constraints for the sake of getting business done; and who are increasingly disinclined to put the institution above their own personal agendas.

I kept a daily journal during the 27 months of my Senate employment. To make what could be a journey of byzantine complexity more manageable, I have decided to explore the events of one work week in the life of the Senate: April 25 through April 29, 1983. This week is emblematic of the Senate at one of the most portentous stages in its existence—that of a legislative body with one foot in the past and one foot in the future, straddling eras and struggling to find an identity.

It was a week both ordinary and extraordinary in the course of the Senate, a week in which momentous issues were considered and none of them resolved; it was thus symptomatic of the kind of organization the Senate has become. It was also a week characteristic of the new era of Republican domination in the Senate, of contemporary methods of wrangling over domestic problems and international entanglements, and of modern White House–Capitol Hill relations, highlighted by a cameo appearance by the President of the United States.

The events of just a single day in the Senate could easily fill the pages of a book. But members never have the leisure to take one day outside the context of another. The five-day, sometimes six, sometimes four-day work week is a popular time frame in the Senate. Many schedules and legislative strategies are weekly, and since most members don't think of Washington, D.C., as home, the working week is often regarded as a roadblock to returning to where they really want to be. A week can also be a convenient line of defense. During an informal press conference at the beginning of the 98th Congress, a reporter asked the majority leader one of the longest questions of his career, running down a lengthy menu of legislative initiatives that might come before a new Congress and inquiring whether the Senate might pass them. The leader gave a deep sigh and pleaded, "Let me just take it a week at a time, will you?"

Any week in the Senate is a week of chaos. To make this tale less chaotic, three senators and three staff members whose careers are emblematic will serve as guideposts. The first, Republican Howard H. Baker, Jr., of Tennessee, then in the twilight of his 17-year Senate career; the second, Alan K. Simpson, Republican of Wyoming and assistant majority leader for the 99th Congress; the third, Democrat Christopher Dodd, from Connecticut. The three staffers are James D. Range, counsel to Baker; Stephen Bell, staff director of the Senate budget committee; and Mary Jane Checchi, an aide to freshman Democratic Senator Frank R. Lautenberg of New Jersey.

Three major issues dominated the business of the Senate and affected the lives of these six players during that week in April: U.S. policy toward Central America, the federal budget, and the reform of immigration laws. These have turned out to be hardy, perennial issues that Congress has shown little sign of being able to master, and they will be the focal points here.

For my cast of characters, the joys and sorrows of Senate life are markedly different than were those of their predecessors. In earlier days, job satisfaction was concentrated among elders who had patiently accumulated respect and influence over the years, and frustration concentrated in the junior ranks where newcomers impatiently discovered how little influence, either on legislation or on the formation of public opinion, they were able to wield.

Now, both satisfaction and frustration are more evenly

shared. The juniors have more opportunity for individual activity and publicity than ever before, because the seniors no longer monopolize the positions of power (which are in any case less powerful). But the frustrations are shared too, and made much worse by the unreal expectations inherited from a past which is gone beyond recall—whether by members, opinion makers, or the constituents who judge them.

The realities of the Senate have changed drastically, but public perceptions and expectations still reflect the conventional wisdom of a generation ago. With this misunderstanding of Congress, and of the Senate in particular, a new era has developed, one characterized by a larger than ever disparity between the expectations that members of Congress bring with them—the expectations of the public—and the new realities of public service, governing and decision making.

Part of the problem is that the Senate, perhaps the most talked-about, written-about, and speculated-about legislative body in the world, is also the most misinterpreted. The Senate is not a collection of transcripts sitting in an archive; there is a powerful human factor. It is all but impossible to capture the motives and traits of 100 individuals with graphs and theories and percentages alone. Eric Redman realized this when he conducted his revealing, authoritative and personal tour of the Senate in *The Dance of Legislation*, but that was more than a decade ago.

The dance goes on, but the music has changed.

1

MONDAY

*It's like running a marathon, but taking three-inch steps
along the way. Probably about a third of the people here
really want to get something done and know how to do it.
Another third want to get something done but don't know
how to do it. And the remaining third, well, I'm not sure why
they're here.*

WARREN RUDMAN (R–N.H.)

Howard Baker likes to sit up front with the chauffeur.
It's not because the majority leader of the United States Senate has such an egalitarian nature, though he does, but because he suffers from car sickness, like a kid, and he thinks
sitting in the back seat only aggravates the symptoms. He
doesn't like arriving at work already dizzy and nauseous. That
can come later.

On a bright, colder-than-usual day in April of 1983, the 56-
year-old Tennessee Republican ambles out of his comfortable
northwest Washington home and heads for the car. The
house he lives in is surprisingly modest, by no means a stately
mansion. Baker doesn't even own it. He and his wife Joy have

been renting it for 17 years. They are residents of Tennessee, and in Washington transients in a transient town.

Greeted with a nod by Wilbur Walker, to whom he once jokingly referred on the Senate floor as "the A.J. Foyt" of government chauffeurs, the majority leader offers morning pleasantries and climbs into the front seat of the government-leased Lincoln Mark IV that Walker has been warming up for him. Walker, wearing the chauffeur's cap that seems by now almost a part of his head, has been driving for various Senate leaders since 1947. For a time he drove Everett McKinley Dirksen, Baker's illustrious father-in-law, when Dirksen was minority leader. The Senate was a different place in those days, Howard Baker knows. An easier place to work, a more manageable place, a place where it wasn't so Herculean a task just to Get Things Done. Howard Baker may wish that those days would come back again, but he knows they never will.

To the north in Maryland, to the south in Virginia, and throughout the District of Columbia, the urban sprawl loosely called Washington awakens to another week. A cover of incongruous calm blankets the city and its suburbs while, at ground level, the chaos and cacophony of Monday rush hour violates the languor of a soft spring morning. Cars crowd the roads and bridges that bring workaday Washingtonians in from the suburbs. Mercedes Benz sedans, Honda Accords, and other varieties in between waddle slowly over Key Bridge from Virginia and down Connecticut Avenue from Maryland. Meanwhile, underground, thousands of commuters fill the city's new, Alphavillian, and perpetually unfinished metro system, many of them stopping first to curse its needlessly complicated, endlessly malfunctioning farecard machines. On television, a local newscaster is giving the average speeds on the main arteries; most hover between a brisk 15 and a zippy 25 miles an hour. As John F. Kennedy said, it's a southern town. Things move slowly here.

In any other city, the great tangle of cars and lumbering metrobuses would be called traffic. But here, inescapably, it is also a metaphor for bureaucracy.

Baker's car pulls out of the driveway and heads down Massachusetts Avenue. Though undeniably big, black, and gas-guzzling, the car is no limousine. Senate leaders used to travel in limousines, but in 1981 the new Republican majority decided to eliminate them as a cost-cutting measure. It was little more than a cosmetic gesture, but thereafter Baker, minority leader Robert Byrd, assistant leaders Ted Stevens (R–Alaska) and Alan Cranston (D–Calif.), and president pro tempore Strom Thurmond (R–S.C.), would make their way about town in shorter, though still chauffeured, cars. Thurmond, at least, had made it known that he longed for the limos of yore.

As he looks out at the stream of cars ahead, Baker chats with Walker, but he is clearly not his usual, buoyant self. He'd been at fashionable Sibley Memorial Hospital over the weekend for tests to determine the cause of a persistently aching stomach. He was so sick he canceled his planned keynote address at the previous Saturday's Statesman's Dinner, one of the biggest fundraising events of the year for the Tennessee GOP. Baker has always hated to cancel a speech, especially one deemed politically important; he hastened to make it up to the crowd at the fundraiser by arranging for President Reagan to speak to them via a telephone hookup.

Although the wire services have erroneously reported over the weekend that doctors had discovered a serious ulcer, the real cause of Baker's pains is a small hole in his stomach lining, brought on by medication he had taken after a knee operation. Much of this day, he has already figured out, will be spent refuting the news accounts and assuring everyone that he is feeling better, and is manifestly ulcerless.

Nobody would have been surprised if it *had* been an ulcer, including Baker himself. The Senate has caused more than its share among those who serve there. It's a veritable breeding ground. An ulcer is an apt response to life in the new Senate, especially for someone who might, by only a slight stretch of terms, be considered an oldtimer. But Baker's worst fears have been dispelled by the tests.

Baker knows, however, that few if any of the matters he

and the Senate will be wrestling with in the week ahead can be resolved so neatly. As the car moves past the manicured chanceries of Embassy Row, Baker sighs, thinking about some of the lions and tigers that await him in the cage. The most ferocious is the federal budget, confounding and complex, as negotiations shutter forward on a resolution for FY84.

In addition, the press has already been speculating that the emotionally charged issue of immigration reform would come before the Senate this week. Baker has not yet figured out how an immigration battle will fit into the Senate schedule, nor does he have a sense of how the bill will be maneuvered through the gauntlet of 99 other individual Senate agendas once it gets to the floor.

And if Chris Dodd of Connecticut—at 39, one of the Senate's youngest members—is going to persist in his demands for a secret session of the Senate on Central America, this will only complicate the week further. That controversy has already been receiving extravagant public and congressional attention, especially because of President Reagan's plan to address a joint session of Congress with a defense of his Central American policy on Wednesday—his first such appearance to deal with a foreign policy matter.

Baker feels no particular personal or political stake in any of these issues; but as pope to Ronald Reagan's God, he will have to be a fixture of stability amid the whirlwind of conflicting positions. Republicans themselves are anything but united on the three issues, to say nothing of the rumblings of opposition being heard from the Democratic ranks. Baker's plan, for the moment, is to stand fast and tall with the president; he hopes the two of them will be able to convince others to come and stand with them.

Five miles southeast of Baker's home, at the U.S. Capitol, the East Front plaza is filling up with cars of congressional staff members, for whom the parking lot is both convenient and free. As usual, a swarm of Capitol police is on duty to admit only those cars with the prized little red parking stickers. In Washington, stratification is something you wear on the bumper of your car—among other places, of course—and to some degree, you are where you park.

Even with several restricted parking locations around the Capitol, and a maze of lots for the House and Senate office buildings, spaces are coveted. Here, rights of residence are like most rights on Capitol Hill: assigned and wangled. Usually parking privileges are part of the deal made at the time of hiring, and experienced negotiators know which lots to shoot for. Changing a staffer's parking location is also a favorite ploy among members; sometimes they use the shift to pat staffers on the back, instead of giving them a raise.

Inside, on the second floor of the Capitol, armed with a cup of coffee and two doughnuts, Mary Kay O'Hara navigates her way through an early-morning tour group in the mammoth rotunda. She is en route to her desk in the majority leader's office—Howard Baker's office—around the corner. At 31, O'Hara is typical of many women on Capitol Hill in that she is single, skillful—and officially subordinate. She is assistant to the counsel for the majority leader and, on paper, this means she is responsible merely for such clerical and secretarial functions as the counsel sees fit. But in reality, because O'Hara has worked on the Hill for nearly ten years, because she is thus among the elite who do understand for the most part what on earth is going on here, and because her boss is very dependent on her, O'Hara is in effect a full-time legislative assistant and unofficial Mother to the Counsel.

The counsel is James D. Range. Jim Range is a legislative cowboy—a southern, tough-talking, Jack Daniels–drinking, boyishly handsome, charismatic lawyer who long ago made the right connections on his way up north. He speaks loudly in an accent that sounds like it belongs to one of the characters in "Deliverance," and he dresses in a style that might be called Macho Bizarro: woven tweed jackets from the preppy and popular Georgetown store Britches, white on white shirts with five-inch collars, and polyester pants pulled up to his chest.

At 36, the blustery Range has become one of a handful of key aides recognized by senators and staff alike as an authoritative source of crucial information about the Senate's agenda. Often, members ask Range questions about the scheduling of bills or votes when they don't want to bother Baker. For a while, Senator Alan Dixon, a Democrat from Illinois, would call Range on sunny mornings to find out if there would be votes that day, and when the Senate would recess. Dixon, an avid golfer, isn't up for reelection until 1986.

Politically, the marriage between Range and his assistant, O'Hara, seems to be one made in hell. O'Hara is to the right of the New Right; Range is, in the minds of many, a closet Democrat. O'Hara's submissiveness to Range bothers some, but not her—perhaps because of her New York Irish upbringing, her strength, her detachment, and her ability to remember that life actually does extend beyond the Hill.

Range and O'Hara like to meet early each morning for breakfast in the Senate dining room. Breakfasting with your secretary isn't typical counsel behavior, but it is typical Range behavior. Mornings are the best time to eat in the "exclusive" dining room on the first floor of the Capitol because it's usually quiet. Those few senators present hide behind their morning papers, while a handful of staff endeavors to impress visitors and friends. For $1.99, one can get the federally subsidized breakfast special: two eggs, toast, hash browns, orange juice, and coffee. O'Hara, who makes $28,000 a year, often has to lend her boss, who makes $59,000 a year, the two bucks for his meal. Range is always short of cash.

But now 8:45 has rolled around, and Range still hasn't materialized. So O'Hara has strolled off to the other side of the Capitol and down to the House "carryout," a cafeteria open to those in need of quick coffee, burnt toast and greasy eggs. A few minutes later, returning to Baker's offices, she hears in the distance a familiar roar. As she walks in, there he is, bumming from another staffer the first of his 30 daily cigarettes, and complaining that O'Hara has kept him waiting to eat. He looks scoffingly at her little cardboard tray of food and tells her, "Honeybunch, you can throw that crap away right now." Range grabs O'Hara's hand and leads her out the door.

Just after 9:00, as his car moves along Constitution Avenue, Baker picks up the phone and rings his personal secretary of eight years, Lura Nell Triplett, to tell her he is on his way in, but is stopping to see Dr. Freeman Carey, the Capitol physician, before coming upstairs to the office. Triplett buzzes staffers on the intercom to tell them the arrival of "the senator" is imminent. Nobody has to be told which senator she means. "The" means Baker. Activity all through Baker's large office begins to pick up.

When Baker was elected minority leader in 1977, a major fringe benefit of the victory was his move from his crowded Senate office building to the spacious, catered, drafty, but rarefied environment of the U.S. Capitol, America's most historic office building. The work that came with those offices would, Baker had learned, sometimes exasperate him, but the physical surroundings offered considerable compensation.

The office is the same one his father-in-law, Everett Dirksen, had occupied for his nine years as minority leader. It is only yards from the Senate floor and offers a postcard-perfect westward view: the Capitol reflecting pool, the mall, and the Washington Monument, which stands like an exclamation point at the end of it. The suites are an open forest of marble and walnut, a palatial, but functional, layout tourists never see. It is Baker's world by choice. No one was shocked when, upon being elected to the post of majority leader when the Republicans won control of the Senate in 1981, Baker chose to stay where he was, leaving Robert Byrd, the Democrat who had gone from majority to minority leader, in the larger offices Baker could have claimed for his own. Baker stayed put not only because of the obvious family ties, but also for the historical ties. The offices are on the site of the original Library of Congress, before it was a separate building; here, in

1812, the British callously set fire to the Capitol. Baker fancies himself a Senate historian, and has been something of a crusader for the preservation and renovation of the Capitol. He loves giving scholarly tours of the building to people who visit him, and retails Senate lore the way others tell family stories.

Baker's journey to the Capitol from Huntsville, Tennessee (pop. 519), reads like a Hollywood screenplay about power struggles, stardom, and romance. Throughout it all, he has remained a political and personal paradox—ideologically eclectic, ambitious yet temperate.

His father, Howard Baker, Sr., served in the House of Representatives for 14 years until his death in 1964. He was succeeded by his second wife, Irene, who served out the rest of his term. While in office, Congressman Baker would send his son copies of the *Congressional Record*, inspiring a fascination with Congress that was, Baker later recalled, "almost immediate."

The young man's attraction to politics was matched only by his attraction to a politician's daughter, and in 1951 Baker married Joy Dirksen, only child of Everett. Howard Jr.'s political future, though, was anything but obvious to his father-in-law. In 1960, Dirksen told a Nixon-for-President rally that John F. Kennedy's only qualification for office was his service on a PT boat, and added, "I have a son-in-law with me tonight who also served on a PT boat in the South Pacific during the war, and I don't hear anyone suggesting he run for anything."

Gradually, however, Baker's impatience with a successful Knoxville law practice began to be taken for what it was: a chafing at the bit for an elective post.

There is little doubt that Baker could have won election to the House when his stepmother retired; the seat was as safe for him as elections get down there. But the upstart had other seats in mind, namely one in the Senate, where no Tennessee Republican had resided since 1913.

Baker lost badly in his first bid for the Senate in 1964, but established a bastion of support for his victory two years later. He entered the Senate in January of 1967 with four other Republicans—Mark Hatfield, Edward Brooke, Clifford Hansen, and Charles Percy—all pegged as young, attractive and ambitious. A bona fide Mod Squad.

None would prove to be as hungry as Baker. In 1969, exhibiting the boldness and fervor that brought him to the Senate in the first place, he decided, to the surprise of many, to challenge Hugh Scott for the right to succeed Dirksen (who had died in office). The results were the same as in 1964: resounding defeat. The race wasn't so much as close; Baker even lost the support of many of his younger colleagues, who regarded his bid as too much too soon. Another defeat at the hands of Scott in 1970 finally slowed him down.

But just for a while. What "congressional brat" status and premature yearnings made difficult for him, that highly publicized, nationally televised question "What did the president know and when did he know it?" made easy. The sudden fame was a bit ironic, since Scott had assigned Baker to the Senate Watergate committee to keep him out of the public eye and thus not be a threat to Scott in a future leadership fight. But, of course, the televised Watergate hearings made Baker's a household face in the living rooms of America. He was the proverbial overnight success. Later, he delivered the keynote address at the 1976 Republican convention in Kansas City, where he was briefly rumored to be Jerry Ford's top choice for vice president. In 1977, a few days before the Senate GOP party caucus was to meet, he entered the race to succeed Scott as minority leader and defeated Robert Griffin of Michigan by one vote.

Behind a door simply marked "private" in Baker's suite, an elegant conference room is filling up with Baker aides and Senate officers. It is almost 9:30, time for the daily leadership meeting over which Baker presides. Morning small talk around the table mostly concerns Baker's health, this being an April Monday and there having been no weekend Redskins game to rehash. Triplett is on the phone explaining to Senator Mack Mattingly of Georgia that Baker has not arrived in the office yet. Since he came to the Senate in 1981, Mattingly has called Baker virtually every morning with the hope of getting an inside track on the day's events. The Baker staff considers the calls something of a nuisance, but Baker has never tried to discourage Mattingly from making them.

As majority leader, Baker is clearly the most powerful member of the Senate. He exacts more deference and exercises more control than any of his colleagues but, as with many aspects of life in the contemporary Senate, being majority leader isn't what it used to be. Widely praised as one of the most effective Senate leaders of this century, Baker nevertheless does not enjoy the control over the membership that many of his predecessors did; senators are younger and bolder now, and more independent, and, perhaps most significantly, both media-wise and media-mad. They are thus less susceptible to blandishments from party leadership. Indeed, an increasing number are virtually immune.

In his 1956 book *Citadel*, William S. White wrote, "The word 'senate' literally means an assembly of old men or elders—a rather apt description of a body that in the late 84th Congress held 15 members of more than 70 years of age (with six of them, indeed, over 75 years of age) and a vast majority who had passed their 60th birthday."

When the 96th Congress convened in 1979, the median age of all members had dropped to 47; 48 of the members were serving in their first term. In the 97th Congress, the number of rookies reached 56, the largest percentage since senators began to be directly elected in 1913; there were now only five members who had passed their 70th birthdays. Between 1961 and 1981, the proportion of senators with more than 11 years of service declined by nearly one half, while at the same time the proportion of newcomers more than doubled.

The seasoned to elderly professional politicians who formerly dominated Senate ranks have been replaced by younger individuals who come to the Senate from diverse walks of life—a basketball player, an astronaut, a haberdasher, an airline pilot, a plywood manufacturer, and so on.

And by the time of the 98th Congress, there were 24 members who had never held an elective office before their election to the United States Senate.

Howard Baker manages a smile as he enters the conference room, looking into each person's face as he is greeted with a "good morning," on occasion poking fun at what he considers an exotic fashion—a loud pair of socks or a racy sportcoat. A mere five feet six inches tall, Baker exudes authority but also a certain shaggy affability, almost as if he were a little boy in grownup's clothing. His dress is conservative-frumpy, and in every outfit there's always one tiny incongruity—a Brooks Brothers gray suit, button-down shirt, and regimental striped tie, but there on his feet, a pair of quirky old buckled shoes that look like they went out of style with The Monkees.

The Baker morning staff meeting establishes direction, sets both short- and long-term agendas, and monitors the concerns and activities of other senators and the White House. For the staff, the meetings represent the best opportunity to observe Baker's decision-making process in action and to learn his private views on upcoming issues. Moreover, since the various individuals are each contributing selected portions of information, the meeting is usually the first time the entire picture for the day is assembled. For Baker the meeting affords the opportunity to determine, early in the day, what he will be faced with in the next 24 hours—what situations, demands, and considerations, both political and procedural, are likely to arise. Baker is not the master of procedure that minority leader Robert Byrd is, but that doesn't bother him. He can conceptualize most of the procedural situations he finds himself involved in, and when he is unsure, he simply calls the parliamentarian and says, "I need to understand what my options are here." In the game of legislative strategy, Baker will entertain lengthy discussions on alternative paths, but he always knows where he wants to wind up. As for agenda-setting, a primary role, it is a tortuous process, dependent on obtaining as much reliable information from as many sources and offices as possible.

When the meetings first began, there were usually six to eight Baker staffers in attendance, along with assistant majority leader Ted Stevens and one or two of his assistants. Now the meetings have ballooned into gatherings of 14, sometimes 18 staffers, all there because Baker likes to be inundated with information. Baker's chief of staff, James Cannon, believing that the meetings had been getting too large but at the same time realizing that he couldn't get Baker to agree to limit their size, had recently begun to organize a smaller second meeting, following the 9:30 get-together, to discuss critical and more private questions of the day.

Baker's interests are protean, his appetite for insights insatiable. A question about Senate Rule 22 on post-cloture filibusters could be followed by a story about an altercation with his home computer; an inquiry into the effectiveness of a new piece of equipment at a breeder-reactor by a discussion of chemical activity in darkroom developing.

Today, as is the case with most of these meetings, those present can be divided into two groups. The first is the active participant group, whose duties place it at the center of policy questions and consultations. The second is more passive, a spectator group that spends its time being attentive. The active group consists of Senator Stevens, Baker chief of staff Cannon, secretary of the Senate William Hildenbrand, secretary for the majority Howard Greene, his assistant John Tuck, Baker's press secretary Tommy Griscom, and Jim Range.

Stevens generally doesn't display much of an interest in the intricacies of the day, but is known in the meetings for his boundless enthusiasm for the Alaska railroad bill and amendments to increase members' pay. He is a serious and stern man, fabled for his temper, but he has generally been loyal to Baker, hoping that such fidelity would help him when he ran for the top spot himself.

Hildenbrand, 61, came to the Senate in 1960, and has been the secretary of the Senate since Baker became majority leader.

Although he is the Senate's chief administrative officer—with a domain that includes 180 aides, a $5.5 million budget, the Senate library, and the parliamentarian's office—it is legislative strategy that enthralls him most, and his frustration with the behavior of newer members (the 77 who arrived in the Senate after he did) is often apparent. Hildenbrand's voice is always the most opinionated at the meetings, as he unloads his views on legislative procedure.

Howard Greene, 38, secretary for the majority, also offers opinions on procedure, because as the actual supervisor of floor operations, it is his responsibility to maintain an up-to-date program of pending legislation. To that end, he keeps a confidential copy of the Senate calendar, with handwritten notations characterizing senators' positions on various issues and their willingness to allow certain legislation to come to the floor for consideration. Greene once admitted that the time his copy of the calendar was missing for seven hours was one of the most terrifying periods of his life.

Greene deals personally with every Republican member of the Senate, but saves his loyalty for Baker. He is known as a man of his word. After hearing complaints from other members at the 9:30 meetings about the foul smell and smoke of the Cuban cigars that Senator Barry Goldwater always managed to smuggle to him, Greene promised to stop smoking, and then adopted the crowd-pleasing practice of simply chewing on the damn things without lighting them.

John Tuck, Greene's assistant, is a navy commander who spends much of his vacation time in the navy reserves. He is one of the few military types around the Capitol in a policy position, and that makes him, his shiny wing-tips and perfectly folded handkerchiefs, stand out. He has a snappy military manner—something that comes in handy when trying to squeeze a word in among all of Hildenbrand's. Tuck's briefings for Baker sound suited for Patton, filled as they are with battlefield metaphors and military jargon. Tuck is the kind of man who cares more about the institution and the process than about the outcome of a particular issue. He's Senate-crazy. He loves it here.

Across from Tuck sits Tommy Griscom, considered by most reporters covering the Senate to be the best and most-listened-to press secretary on the Hill. Griscom's office, twenty feet from Baker's, has become a home away from home for many correspondents. There are two reasons: first, any action taking place in the Senate invariably involves the majority leader; and second, Griscom has made a practice of sharing as much as he can, both on and off the record, with the press.

And at the far end of the long table booms Range, perpetually puffing away on a cigarette, the only man present in shirt sleeves. Range spends the meetings advocating a carefully designed agenda of his own and making short chatty notes to himself that he decorates with hand-drawn stars.

Baker has his hands full keeping track of his colleagues' plots, schemes, and moods. It is Range's job to keep Baker up to date on as many of the over 5,000 Senate staff members as necessary. Baker knows he can't get the full picture just talking to senators; staffers play an enormous role. Range makes it his habit to inform Baker on which staffers are most influential with their chiefs. He is famous, too, for his unrelenting pursuit of information that staffers do not want revealed. Once he pries it out of them—often before they've told their own bosses—he can brief Baker on a member's strategy well before the staffer does. Before a bill comes to the floor, Range will meet privately with the staff director of that committee to ascertain the game plan and make sure it coincides with the leader's.

This morning's meeting has barely come to order when the buzzer sounds on Baker's phone; it is the minority leader, Robert Byrd, calling. Baker and Byrd usually talk by phone in the early morning to probe one another about impending business; both have had so much experience in the relationship that they almost never give away more information than they want to. Byrd is calling this morning about young Senator Christopher Dodd's request for a secret session of the Senate on Nicaragua. Baker, mindful that both the White House and the majority of his colleagues, especially intelligence committee chairman Goldwater, are opposed to the briefing, asks Byrd, "Can he be talked out of this?" Those at the meeting can tell from the look on Baker's face that Byrd's reply is not encouraging. Hildenbrand, the secretary of the Senate, asks Baker, "Is there a second?", referring to the Senate rule requiring at least two members to petition for such a session. But Baker is just hearing from Byrd that Paul Tsongas, Democrat of Massachusetts, has agreed to second Dodd's motion. Grudgingly, Baker informs Byrd that the session will be held the following afternoon, per Dodd's request; this will give Capitol security forces time to "sweep" the Senate chamber in the morning for bugging devices. As soon as Baker hangs up the phone, Range growls, "It's a piece-of-shit move to embarrass the president." Range has a knack for saying bluntly what many are thinking quietly.

Thus begins Howard Baker's week: two freshman minority senators dictate a major change in the Senate's schedule, and the majority leader is unable to do anything to stop them.

Chief of staff Cannon asks, "Do you want me to tell Duberstein?", referring to Ken Duberstein, the White House congressional liaison director. Baker says "Thank you," meaning yes. The problem for the White House is that the president had wanted to deal a preemptive strike on the Central America issue. The week before, the White House had requested time for a policy speech by President Reagan before a joint session of Congress—and, of course, a national prime-time television audience. But joint sessions require the passage of a resolution in both houses of Congress; the House had put off voting on the request until some time after the weekend. Word had it that Speaker O'Neill had finally found an opportunity to play golf at the celebrated Augusta Country Club in Georgia, home of the Masters; he wasn't going to miss the chance to do that just for a joint session of Congress to help Ronald Reagan. The delay in the president's speech would prove to be a great boon for Dodd.

Howard Greene, the secretary for the majority, brings up

the next item on the agenda—an extended summer recess—which is met with laughter around the room. Normally, the Senate gets down to business the last week of January, after the president's State of the Union address. From then on, the Senate is in session when the Senate is in session—and out of session as often as the senators can swing it. Ernest Hollings of South Carolina described a Senate year this way: "In January, we wait to get the president's budget, then there's the Lincoln and Washington birthday recess, then we're off for the spring holidays—Easter and Memorial Day—then we're off for the Fourth of July, then we're off for the summer, and then Labor Day, and then, of course, Thanksgiving and Christmas. If I were king for a day, I'd have to tell everybody that the honeymoon was over and that we aren't organized for the purpose of finding out what holidays we can go home on."

"You've got some crazies loose, leader, over this July and August recess business," Greene says. "Why don't you just announce the go-ahead?" Greene is trying to determine the prospects for extending, as previously proposed, the summer recess from Memorial Day to Labor Day. Baker cracks a smile; although he considers the plan to be consistent with his goal for making members "citizen legislators" who spend most of their time back home, he knows that Greene, and undoubtedly Hildenbrand as well, are thinking about their travel plans for the recess. When the Senate is out of session, most at this meeting are out of town. Hildenbrand is usually heading a delegation of members to some exotic place around the globe; and Greene, if he isn't joining Hildenbrand, is prominently planted on a golf course.

"It probably won't fly," Baker says, and with good reason. The prospects for the extension look increasingly grim because work on appropriation bills is proceeding slowly, and it would be, in Baker's judgment, political and institutional suicide to recess the Senate without action on the majority of the spending bills. The Constitution declares that "no money shall be drawn from the Treasury but in Consequence of Ap-

34

propriations made by law." This power is held exclusively by the legislative branch; procedurally, the House originates all appropriation bills. If Congress fails to provide funds through an appropriation bill, then a continuing resolution is adopted to serve as a stop-gap funding measure. Continuing resolutions can't continue forever; failure to renew or pass the appropriate appropriation bills could actually shut down the federal government, which has nearly happened more than once in recent years. The plan at present, Baker decides, should be to turn the tables on the House; Baker says that the Senate should make it clear that the summer recess will be delayed unless the House starts sending over the bills in a more timely fashion than has been the case since the Republicans took control of the Senate.

The message travels across the room. For Tommy Griscom, part of his spiel to the press today will be that the Senate is once again being delayed by the House; that the failure to act on spending measures—thus forcing the government to rely further on continuing resolutions for the money necessary to keep operating—is bad economic policy; and that the Senate majority leader is anxious to dispose of bills quickly, but can't because he hasn't received any. Baker tells Jim Range, and Daniel Crippen, his in-house economic advisor, "Get Tommy a list showing dates of appropriation bills received from the House during the past two years." Chief of staff Cannon says he will inform Duberstein at the White House of this move as well.

The basic flow of legislation has not changed dramatically in the United States. The most common path starts with the introduction of a bill by a member, usually through a statement on the Senate floor during morning business hours. The bill is then referred, according to the parliamentarian's judgment of precedents, to the committee of predominant jurisdiction. After that ruling is made, the committee will, at some stage, hold hearings on the measure, inviting testimony from interested and affected parties. Mark-up is the next hurdle, where language is drafted and any committee amendments to the bill are offered and voted on. After the votes, the committee then reports the bill out, usually with a committee report that describes the purposes of the legislation and its estimated cost; the report may also include a summary of the views of those who voted against the bill in committee. This report is then printed by the U.S. Government Printing Office. Once the report has been available to members for 72 hours, the accompanying bill is eligible for floor consideration, and the jockeying for floor time begins.

Most bills are called up for debate on the floor by unanimous consent, a device which circumvents cumbersome procedural rules. "Unanimous consent" does not mean everyone agrees; it means only that no one objects. If such consent cannot be obtained, a debatable motion to consider the bill is offered. If that motion is agreed to, the bill becomes the pending business and the amendment process begins on the floor. When these votes on the amendments are over, the Senate as a whole votes on the bill in its current form. If it is a bill that has originated in the Senate, then once the bill is passed it will be sent over to the House for consideration there. The House may pass its own version of the bill, as it commonly does, and then the process of conference, or "marrying up" the differences between the two chambers, begins. This conference is charged with achieving perfect accord on a mutual bill. House members are traditionally thought to be better in conference negotiations than senators; they develop expertise because their time is not spread so thin over so many issues, the result of fewer committee assignments. Once the conference agrees to a bill, the conference reports are sent back to each chamber for a vote. If the new compromise package is passed in the House and the Senate, it is then sent to the president, whose signature, if he approves the bill, will make it law.

More than two dozen items of legislation are now awaiting action by the full Senate, having been reported from committees. Every one of them has at least a committee chairman and a group of supporting senators urging Baker to put it on the schedule. Each week Baker is faced with the task of scheduling Senate floor time in order to meet those requests; it is a losing battle. Bills cannot be disposed of quickly enough in order for everything to be considered. Baker's big-ticket item at the moment is the FY84 budget resolution, which was reported out of the budget committee the previous week. But because of a Senate rule that requires three days to expire between committee approval and the beginning of consideration on the floor of the Senate, the resolution cannot be ready until the beginning of the following week. Baker could try to waive the rule, but chooses not to; he needs this week to get the Republican house in order.

"If you take that bear up next Monday," Howard Greene tells Baker, "you can go with your promise to Simpson this week." Baker's promise—to immigration subcommittee chairman Alan Simpson, Republican of Wyoming—was that deliberations will begin on the immigration bill this week. "What about Thurmond?" Baker asks, referring to the judiciary chairman, who has been pressing the case for action this week on a bankruptcy reform bill. Jim Range answers: "You can get to both of 'em."

Immigration is a big problem for Baker; it's highly controversial and riddled with the kinds of intricacies that stymie the process. The Republican controlled Senate had passed an immigration bill the previous year, but the House failed to approve it, and the end of the Congress in 1982 nullified the Senate action. Simpson, the warrior of immigration legislation, started from square one again this year, and made better time, with greater success than most expected. Baker had told Simpson all along that, when he got his bill out of committee, he'd get his day in court, or rather on the Senate floor. The judiciary committee had passed the bill on April 18, but in the last few days, as a result of reports from Range and in conversations with other members, Baker was starting to get a little uneasy about the bill. Baker told Simpson he'd heard that there were "all types of amendments out there." Simpson knew what this meant; that he should work out as many of the disagreements as possible behind the scenes before the bill got to the floor and became Baker's burden. To help the matter along, Simpson began looking for possible time agreements with other senators, which would limit debate on the bill to manageable levels.

Since Tuesday will be lost to the secret session, Baker already feels he is falling behind. He asks Greene and Range to propose a suggested agenda consistent with his commitments. "Poke around and see if we can get bankruptcy up and out of here on Wednesday, then take care of Simpson on Thursday," he says.

Triplett buzzes to let Baker know that budget committee chairman Pete Domenici is waiting for him in the outer office. Baker hangs up the phone and says, "Domenici's outside. Thank you, gentlemen." The week is now by and large mapped out. The only thing that will interfere with the schedule now is the reality of life in the modern Senate.

Senator Pete Domenici, Republican of New Mexico, lopes into the conference room and greets those assembled with a robust hello. At his side, not surprisingly, is Steve Bell, the staff director of the budget committee. Bell not only manages and administers the staffing affairs of the committee, but serves as the chairman's confidant and sidekick.

The Baker claque begins to file out the door, except for Range and chief of staff Cannon. Range begins chatting with Bell. Since Ronald Reagan was elected, the two of them have become the most important staff members in the Senate on the subject of budget deliberations. Domenici says to Baker, "You know I feel like I've already been through a war," referring to his committee's deliberations on next year's budget resolution, "but I realized this morning that the big battle hasn't even started."

Every budget resolution is incredibly complex, and as a result produces fierce debate and frustration.

Prior to 1974, Congress relied mainly on the president to lend unity and coherence to federal budgeting. Under the

Budget and Accounting Act of 1921, each year the president has submitted a comprehensive budget that embraces the spending and taxing plans of the federal government. For many years, Congress acted on the president's recommendations by referring bits and pieces of his overall plan to various congressional committees. Each committee reviewed the recommendations referred to it and produced appropriate legislation, largely according to its own desires and its own timetable. In a sense, what the president put together, Congress pulled apart. While the budgetary role of the president, in theory, emphasized developing new initiatives, integrating them into a complete plan, and marshalling political support for legislative action, Congress' budgetary role was characterized by fragmentation, delay, and occasionally inaction.

By 1973, Congress had decided to reform—to devise, in essence, a *congressional* budget process. It sought a means of annually deciding overall budgetary and economic policy as a first step, and then considering individual spending and tax measures to carry out the budget plan. To this end, Congress passed the Congressional Budget and Impoundment Control Act of 1974, which President Nixon signed into law on July 12, 1974, less than a month before he left office. The act provided Congress with the means of enunciating a fiscal policy and setting spending priorities through the annual adoption of two or more "concurrent resolutions" on the budget.

Each spring, allegedly, the congressional budget process begins with the adoption of a first budget resolution—setting targets for total revenues, spending, the deficit or surplus, and the level of the public debt. Budget resolutions do not affect the budget directly, since they do not become law. Rather, they enable Congress to establish guidelines for the consideration of separate tax bills, appropriations, and other budget-related measures.

A second budget resolution (when not tied to the first) is adopted in the fall, and provides Congress with an opportunity to reaffirm or revise the policies set in the first resolution. Where the first resolution is advisory, and is meant to guide but not predetermine legislative action, the second resolution establishes binding ceilings on spending and a floor under revenues. It all sounds very orderly but, as in many cases, what is a pristine schematic on paper becomes acrimonious bedlam when the Senate actually begins to grapple with the problems.

To help the Congress along, the budget act also created three new entities—House and Senate budget committees and the Congressional Budget Office (CBO). The House and Senate budget committees have responsibility for reporting and enforcing budget resolutions. Additionally, the budget committees oversee the CBO and study budget-related matters. The CBO supports Congress by providing budgetary analyses and information. During each budget cycle, CBO analyzes the president's budget, prepares reports on budget options and alternatives, issues periodic scorekeeping reports on the budgetary impact of legislation, and estimates the five-year costs of all spending measures. Many members regard the CBO as a vital element in the new congressional budget process—affording Congress independent and nonpartisan expertise, and thereby lessening Congress's reliance on the president's Office of Management and Budget and the executive agencies. Unlike rosy White House projections, CBO figures are more realistic and, as a result, more respected.

It is only April, but Baker, Domenici, Range, and Bell have been through what seems to them an entire decade since the beginning of the year.

The plan for the FY84 budget, as devised by both the White House and the Republican leadership in the Senate, had been to move as quickly as possible, thus reporting a Senate plan out before the House budget committee could act.

Bell had optimistically marked on Domenici's calendar a target date for reporting out the first resolution on March 15. He had even, in typical Bell fashion, penned on the schedule a press conference to be held afterward.

After the State of the Union address, Ken Duberstein, the White House liaison man, scheduled a breakfast meeting in the president's living quarters in the White House. Attending were himself, National Security Council advisor William Clark, chief of staff Jim Baker, and the Republican Senate six-pack—Howard Baker, Domenici, Paul Laxalt of Nevada, Jake Garn of Utah, Mark Hatfield of Oregon, and Robert Dole of Kansas. Conspicuously absent were assistant majority leader Ted Stevens and armed services chairman John Tower, both staunch defenders of budget increases for the Department of Defense.

Defense expenditures turned out to be the talk of the day. Garn, who described himself over breakfast that morning as a "superhawk," spoke in the only manner he knows—strongly—about the need to cut proposed defense budget increases to win the budget fight. Howard Baker reported that he could see no possible way of passing the double-digit increase for defense the president wanted.

The meetings continued after the president's budget was submitted on January 31, 1983. It still included a double-digit hike in defense, as well as politically difficult domestic spending cuts, and no significant increases in taxes. It projected a fiscal year 1984 budget deficit of $175 billion, the biggest reason for both the laughter and tears it was met with on the Hill. The president's budget arrived in Congress a virtual orphan.

On March 7, two days before the opening session of Pete Domenici's budget committee, Domenici told the president that there was little support for the proposed budget, especially for the numbers on defense. He also told his committee, and had Bell tell the press, that there would be a delay in consideration of the defense and revenue issues, allegedly because it was difficult to get members to show up at the committee meetings. The committee and the press understood the message perfectly: the administration had asked for more time to get its act together.

The Democrats on the committee cried foul. They argued that the White House was attempting to dominate the budget process and preempt the Congress, and that the delay would mean there would be more time for a public relations campaign to be waged against the proposed cuts in defense. The administration denied such intentions, but did alert the White House speech writing team to the possibility that the president might be making a televised "report to the nation" on the country's efforts to keep pace with the military aggressiveness of the Soviet Union.

At the opening session of the mark-up, Domenici focused his remarks on the need for compromise—a theme that Bell had written into the speech not only for his boss's sake, but also, as he put it later, for "Baker's and Reagan's." Bell was suspicious of the president and Secretary of Defense Caspar Weinberger from the start; now he was growing suspicious of the majority leader as well. He felt that Baker had changed the equation on Domenici, from "get me a budget that the majority of Republicans can support" to "get me a budget that the majority of Republicans and the president can support."

As of March 12, five days after Domenici's initial delaying tactic, there was still no statistical revision from the White House on its original budget. Ken Duberstein and Jim Baker at the White House told Domenici that more time was needed. Domenici, somewhat embarrassed, and increasingly impatient, announced a three-week delay in consideration of the defense and revenue figures.

Bell was incensed. He had urged Domenici to go ahead with the mark-up and was depressed by the reputation his committee was developing in the press and the rest of the Senate. Though he was dedicated and protective of his chairman, he had found himself in a rare position: losing an argument to his boss.

Meanwhile, the Democrats were taking advantage of the delay to promote their own plan—kill the third year of Reagan's 1981 tax cut, repeal the indexing of taxes for inflation, and lower the defense increase to 5 percent. The ranking Democratic member of the budget committee, Lawton Chiles of Florida, was beginning to see rends in the Republican fabric.

On April 5, Domenici and Weinberger met, and the secretary of defense told the chairman that the nation simply couldn't settle for anything less than a 10 percent increase. After hearing this, Domenici brought the Republican members of the budget committee downtown to the White House to meet with the president. It was obvious to all present that there was little support on the committee for the president's desired combination of defense increases and decreasing tax rates. Twenty-four hours later, Domenici was again back at the White House, this time in the company of Chiles. Together, they told the president that they wanted to negotiate, and that he had "little support" in the committee.

Thursday, April 7, turned out to be one of those days that try political souls.

Howard Baker began the day by telling Ken Duberstein what he had been telling him and the rest of the White House staff for weeks: "You have to give Pete some leeway, he can't hold off much longer." At the White House that morning, Baker even repeated it to the president, telling him in absolute terms that a 10 percent increase in defense spending just wouldn't fly.

After consulting with Range and legislative assistant Crippen, and in desperation, Baker offered a budget package that included a 7.5 percent increase for defense; Duberstein dubbed it the "Baker compromise." Reagan directed Jim Baker and David Stockman to see if the administration could buy it; Stockman went to work presenting the new figures to Weinberger's analysts. Jim Baker called Weinberger and recommended accepting the offer. Weinberger said he'd get back to Baker. Meanwhile the majority leader went back to the Capitol, but said he would need an answer by noon if he was going to make the new plan survive.

Noon came and went, but still no word from the Pentagon that the secretary of defense had signed off on the new figure. The budget committee began its meeting at 2:00 P.M. Still, nothing from the Pentagon.

Jim Baker, Stockman, White House presidential assistant

Richard Darman, and Duberstein waited in the chief of staff's office for the call from Weinberger. Jim Baker tried to phone Bill Clark to see if he knew what Weinberger was up to and where, but the NSC chief was not in his office. He was downtown, speaking at a forum sponsored by columnists Rowland Evans and Robert Novak.

Duberstein, aware that Domenici was moving rapidly toward the vote on the defense numbers, convinced Jim Baker to call Weinberger and get the signoff at 7.5 percent. Weinberger's office reported that he would return the call shortly. Howard Baker called to ask what on earth was going on, and to say that he didn't even know now if he could pull off the 7.5 figure; time was running out.

Jim Baker left at this point because he, too, was scheduled to speak at the Evans and Novak political forum. Darman and Duberstein left Baker's office—and saw Weinberger, who, it turned out, had been sitting in the West Wing lobby of the White House all along, with a friend who was scheduled to have his photo taken with the president before going off to be a foreign ambassador. The duo pressed Weinberger for his answer, and Weinberger told them that he and Clark had decided that the president should call Domenici and insist on the 10 percent figure.

Duberstein pleaded that they first call Howard Baker to tell him of their plan. Duberstein called Baker from outside the Oval Office, and asked him whether Baker or the president should transmit the message. Baker replied that he would do it, if he had to, but said he didn't think it would do any good. Baker didn't want the president to put himself on the line, only to be turned down.

Over at the budget committee hearing, Range, whom Baker had deployed to keep an eye on things, checked with Bell to see if things were as grim as Range thought them to be. Bell said that they were going ahead, and Range wouldn't like what he saw. Range called Baker and told him the news. Baker told Range that Domenici might be getting a call from the president to hold off.

Back at the White House, Duberstein told Clark and Weinberger that there was almost nothing encouraging in his conversation with Howard Baker, that things were fairly hopeless. The two men heard him out and then said that they wanted to see the president anyway. Five minutes later in the Oval Office, they told Reagan in the most urgent way they knew that time was running out and that Domenici was disobeying his orders. They appealed to Reagan's image of himself as a strong leader by reminding him that he is the commander in chief, the head gipper, and all that; and Weinberger finally budged, saying that the absolute lowest defense increase he could possibly tolerate would be 7.9 percent.

Duberstein again called Howard Baker in the Republican cloakroom. The conversation was short. Baker said that he thought that this particular card "had already been played." Domenici was unstoppable. Reagan asked his secretary to get Domenici on the phone. When the call came through, Range ran over and whispered in Domenici's ear that the president wanted him on the phone. Reagan told Domenici that he was sure that the chairman was not the problem; it had to be some other rascally Republican on the committee. Sweat running down his cheeks, Domenici informed the president that he was, indeed, part of the problem. Range was standing at Bell's side outside the booth, just watching.

After Reagan calmly told Domenici that, in the national interest and in the name of a strong defense, he should "hold off," Clark, Weinberger, Duberstein, and Darman watched the president scowl and turn crimson; the voice on the other end of the phone was clearly holding fast. The president, uncharacteristically for him, even cursed. But Domenici would not budge. Duberstein wrote the numbers 7.5 and 7.9 on a White House notepad, held it up for the president to see, and held his thumb and forefinger, about an inch apart, in front of the president's face. The president took the cue and told Domenici that the differences were so slight, so close—couldn't Domenici hold off again?

A few seconds later, the president hung up the phone,

slamming the receiver down with such force that it bounced out of the cradle. He was not smiling. He did not look pleased. The conversation was over.

Domenici came out after the phone call and told Bell and Range about the conversation. He asked them what they thought. Bell told his boss that he did the right thing and that they had better get on with the vote. In a loud voice that lifted heads across the hearing room, the chairman announced, "The clerk will call the roll." Range ran and phoned Baker.

What the majority leader and the chairman and the White House legislative liaison team had been saying all along that month was now proving to be accurate. First came the vote on the president's 10 percent figure for defense; the vote was 19–2 against; only Republicans John Tower of Texas and Steven Symms of Idaho voted with the president. Then came the vote to cut the proposed increase from 10 percent to 5 percent; that vote passed by a margin of 17 to 4. Republicans Domenici, Gorton, Armstrong, Kassebaum, Quayle, Andrews, Boschwitz, and Kasten took their biggest steps away from Reagan since he had taken office. Domenici ended the session with a public expression of hope that the bipartisanship displayed that day would continue when the revenue issue was being debated.

Four days later, on April 11, the budget committee, across party lines, rebuffed the president again, adding more than $11 billion to domestic spending, and thus eliminating most of the administration's planned savings on the domestic side.

Meanwhile, it was clear to one and all that, on the issue of revenue, no proposal so far advanced had enough votes to win. The plan put forward by ranking Democrat Chiles would in essence eliminate the third year of Reagan's tax cut and repeal tax indexing. Domenici's own scheme, close to the president's, called for minimal tax increases in 1984 and 1985, but larger ones, totaling $190 billion, in 1986, 1987, and 1988. Bell, ever a believer more in process than in politics, convinced Domenici to cut with Chiles a secret deal that would

46

ensure that the revenue issue didn't prevent the committee from reporting out a resolution. The deal was basically this: if neither Domenici's revenue plan nor Chiles's plan passed, Chiles would offer his compromise plan again, and Domenici would then vote for it.

Bell went to his typewriter and wrote remarks for Domenici for the beginning of the revenue debate. The Democrats, he said, were toying around with the economic recovery now clearly under way; major taxes would simply jeopardize the economy's comeback. The Republicans, meanwhile, he wrote, were going to have to wake up to the realization that the deficit couldn't be cut just by decreasing domestic spending. Domenici gave Bell's speech verbatim in committee the next day.

On April 14, the committee voted, first on the Chiles revenue plan. That measure was defeated on a tie vote of 11 to 11, with all the Democrats sticking together and Republican Mark Andrews of North Dakota joining them.

Now it was Domenici's turn. His plan failed, 8 to 14, with six hard-core, no-tax Republicans deserting their chairman.

The following week, the administration's big guns—Ed Meese, Jim Baker, and David Stockman—finally came to the Hill to offer a compromise: 7.5 percent for defense growth; $136 million more for domestic spending; and minimal increases in taxes. Bell was not impressed, and made sure Domenici knew it. Range told Howard Baker the plan had come too late.

On April 21, what many had come to think was never going to happen, happened. First the committee voted on the president's budget plan: it was defeated, 10 to 6. But then, in accordance with Domenici and Chiles's secret deal, the committee approved a version of the Chiles revenue plan it had previously rejected, by a vote of 12 to 4; that one was followed by a budget resolution in similar terms, reported out, at long last, by a vote of 13 to 4.

Again, Jim Range had to call Howard Baker from the budget committee room with bad news. Baker just sighed. Weeks and weeks of wrangling had come to an end, but it really wasn't the end of anything. Hassles over the budget begin anew when the fight leaves the committee and makes its way to the Senate floor; on the floor, after all, there are even more cooks for the stew. Baker, as the leader, knew that all the passion and rage that went into the committee's fight would be old news when the full debate began. All the players in the drama had to go back to scene one and start over again.

The Senate majority leader was exhausted by the prospect. He felt as though he had spent three weeks running in place. Two months earlier, Baker had announced his intention to retire. With the scars of yet another budget battle still fresh, the prospect of leaving the Senate looked more inviting than ever.

In his office this Monday morning with Domenici, Range, and Bell, Baker is fully aware that the FY84 budget has already shaped up as the most harrowing, difficult, and divisive episode that the Republican majority in the Senate and the Republican president have yet had to deal with, and the biggest test since 1974 of the viability of the budget process.

Domenici knows that he and Baker face a tough fight on the Senate floor. Domenici is now trying to bring the party together—not just to pass a budget resolution but, in Domenici's eyes, to save the budget process itself from imminent chaos. He knows that he and Baker have only this week to pull it off. It won't be easy. Senator Slade Gorton of Washington, looking at the struggle over FY84, had declared, "1981 was the president's year, 1982 was the Senate's year, and 1983 is the year of living dangerously."

Even though there is still an hour to go before Baker travels to the Senate floor for the opening of the Senate at noon, preparations are now under way for the day's session. Outside, Ann Kurtz Haldeman, youngest daughter of former White House chief of staff H. R. Haldeman, hurriedly skips up the white stone steps of the Capitol, five minutes late for work.

As one of 43 Senate doorkeepers, her job is to make sure visitors refrain from talking, taking pictures, reading, or writing while seated in the gallery. It has to do with Senate decorum. Haldeman jumps into a ladies' room for one last adjustment of her Laura Ashley skirt and then reports for duty.

Downstairs, tucked away off the Senate reception area, the Republican cloakroom, another Baker hangout, is beginning to hum. An L-shaped area of no more than 200 square feet, with large leather couches and eight private phone booths, the cloakroom is supposed to be a private gathering place for senators, convenient to, but isolated from, the Senate floor. But the cloakroom has become decreasingly private in the last ten years, because of the large increases in Senate staffs. Now members, when they really want to talk privately—or take a nap—go off to the "Marble Room," behind the Senate chamber, which is open only to the privileged 100.

John Doney, 24, one of the three cloakroom desk assistants, is on the phone answering another inquiry about the upcoming schedule. Both the Republican and Democratic cloakrooms act as nerve centers for the members' offices—relaying information about which bills will be considered for the week, and when votes will occur. J.D., as everyone calls him, has been at work since 9:00; his first order of business was the daily attendance check: which Republican senators will be in town for the day? The tally, 46 out of 54, was rushed to secretary for the majority Howard Greene at the morning leadership meeting in Baker's office. Attendance often plays a big role in the scheduling of close votes.

An hour earlier, the 13 GOP pages had arrived from their classes at the Capitol Page School. Many run around the Capitol and Senate office buildings as messengers, others work on the floor, straightening out each senator's desk in the same fashion: bill reports are placed in the upper right-hand corner of the small cherry-wood desktops and, to their side, a copy of the latest *Congressional Record* and the Calendar of Business. As the noon convening hour nears, J.D. dispatches a page to the Senate sergeant at arms to retrieve the Bible and gavel that are used in the opening ceremony of the Senate, and sends two pages out to put glasses of water on Baker's and Byrd's desks.

The Senate chamber is not only significantly smaller than the House of Representatives chamber, it is considerably more regal. The 100 desks fill the room, which is 125 feet wide and bisected by an aisle that separates the Democrats from the Republicans. The floor is on five different levels, sloping down toward the front of the room where the two leaders reside. In front of them, between Byrd's and Baker's desks and the rostrum, lies the well, a small area at the heart of the chamber where members congregate during votes. The royal blue pattern on the carpet is well worn, and parts of the floor creak with age. Above all this hangs, majestically, a translucent dome decorated with a huge eagle and the Senate seal.

As high noon approaches, visitors in the galleries are able to see the first signs of life on the floor, as the cast files into the chamber below. At each door leading into the chamber, two pages are posted. Their job at this moment is to open the door whenever a member approaches. On this particular day, they will hardly be run ragged doing that.

In the well, properly credentialed members of the press make the only floor appearance they are permitted for the day, gathering around the leaders' desks for the daily "dugout" session—an informal get-together usually held five to ten minutes before the Senate goes into session—so that reporters hungry for their first news opportunities of the day can pelt Baker and Byrd with questions.

As usual, Byrd arrives in the chamber before Baker, and the press drifts over toward him. When Baker shows up five minutes later, the group pounces across the aisle and reporters begin competing with one another for Baker's attention. On this day, most of the questions concern the first concurrent budget resolution, and the president's upcoming address on Central America. "Do you support Senator Dodd's request for the closed session?" one reporter asks Baker. "It's within his rights" is Baker's terse reply.

At five minutes before noon, Strom Thurmond, all 81 years

of him, wanders into the chamber and can be seen puttering around the Senate floor, shaking any and all hands within reach, and not in a namby-pamby way, either, but with a firm, confident grip. As the president pro tempore of the Senate, it is Thurmond's role to bring the Senate to order each day, and while past presidents pro tem have not taken this duty very seriously, Thurmond does. His record of attendance for the openings is almost perfect. He wants to be there to do it himself.

The visitors seated in the gallery all have their own reasons for being where they are at the moment. Typically, some are students, some are tourists, some are constituents who have been ensconced there for the moment by a senator's aide. What they all probably share is an expectation that something of at least fleeting importance is about to happen on the floor below—perhaps fiery debate on the nuclear freeze, or passionate colloquy on the economy. Maybe some even unconsciously expect to watch James Stewart as Mr. Smith making a desperate last stand against party bosses from back home. What they are about to observe today, however, will prove to be something rather less than momentous.

Precisely at noon, Thurmond bangs the gavel and brings the Senate to order. It doesn't take much banging since he, Baker, and Byrd are the only senators present on the floor. Pages stand motionless at their posts at the sound of the gavel. Reporters peer down from the press gallery. Then Thurmond intones in his thick South Carolina accent: "Under the previous order, the Senate will stand in adjournment until 2:00 P.M. on Tuesday, April 26, 1983." He bangs the gavel again and walks off. The entire episode has lasted 12 seconds. Today's session is over.

Around the floor, the cast, such as it is, departs quickly. Pages pick up from Baker's and Byrd's desks the glasses of water that had been so carefully placed there ten minutes earlier. Upstairs in the galleries, some visitors look mildly shocked, probably unaware that the proceedings they have just seen were a technicality, required by Senate rules. According to official Senate procedure, "The Senate may not adjourn for more than three days without the consent of the House of Representatives." If Thurmond hadn't gaveled the day's session in and out, the Senate could have been considered in adjournment.

By the time Baker leaves the chamber, his press secretary, Tommy Griscom, has begun a press conference, adjacent to the big Ohio clock that stands like a grandfatherly sentinel outside the entrance to the Senate chamber. Baker has often complained, jokingly, that Griscom attracts bigger crowds of reporters for his little briefings than Baker does with his own dugout sessions and, indeed, some days he does. Griscom, as a *New York Times* profile reported the previous week, can say things, especially off-the-record things, that Baker cannot. The reporters huddle around him, asking for the "real" line on what is going to happen concerning the budget; when Baker will go to the White House to discuss the problems with the president; and what the prospects of success are for the embattled immigration bill. Griscom cues them in on which senators will be playing key roles in the next few days, and who will be mere supporting players. His raps run the gamut from a rundown of the day's schedule to an explanation of why a photo opportunity can't be set up to detailed discussions of budget provisions. Every so often, Baker drops in just to ascertain the "spin" on what it was he said only moments earlier in the dugout session.

Back in the leader's office, workers from the Senate restaurant are hurriedly draping an institutional-white tablecloth on the conference table in preparation for the leadership luncheon. Fresh fruit and little salads wait to be placed on the table. Earlier this morning, Baker has told Triplett that he doesn't want the normal ample lunch; he is still trying to lose weight. Instead, he has asked her to mix a batch of the Cambridge diet drink that he occasionally uses. Yet, by lunchtime, the good intentions have been replaced by a yearning for real food. Baker will eat the same grub as everyone else.

Each Monday, Baker sits down with his leadership group to

discuss the week ahead. Others present for these get-togethers are Ted Stevens, Strom Thurmond, Senator James McClure of the Republican conference; Senator Tower, chairman of the Republican policy committee; Senator Richard Luger, chairman of the Republican senatorial campaign committee; Senator Garn, secretary of the conference; and Senator Paul Laxalt, who doesn't hold an official title but serves a clear purpose as the president's well-known best friend in Congress.

One of the hottest stories following election night in 1980 was that Laxalt would challenge Baker for majority leader. The rumor appeared to be the not-so-secret desire of those on the far right to have this new Republican majority led by one closer to the new president and closer to the conservative members who pushed the Republicans over the top. So one of Howard Baker's first phone calls after the results were in that election night was to Laxalt, to find out if he was planning to run against him.

While many on the outside thought Laxalt would decide to oust Baker, most Senate insiders didn't give the rumor much credence. Although Laxalt enjoys his celebrity status and close relations with Reagan, he is not well disposed toward the vagaries of procedure, the endless infighting, and the long hours on the Senate floor that come with the majority leader's job. Laxalt lavishes little time on legislative logistics. He's a strong conservative, like his old friend in the White House. His appearances on the Senate floor are rare, usually just for votes, although his entrance in three-button, perfectly tailored suits, and cowboy boots rumored to cost in the thousands, invariably attract the attention of fellow members. He loves to hold court at his back-row desk, where colleagues, including his politically incompatible yet friendly chum Teddy Kennedy, stop by to visit and chat. Laxalt's is not the dynamic for a post such as majority leader, and to his credit he knows it, and knew it when he told Baker he wouldn't run.

Baker and Laxalt had had their differences during the debate on the Panama Canal Treaty, but their relationship had flourished since 1981. Laxalt had become particularly important on those tough trips to the White House during which Baker had to inform the president of bad news: impending legislative defeat, threats of mutiny or defection from the faithful, and requests that the White House change its position on an issue. Laxalt served as a counterbalance, so that when the president looked at bad-tidings Baker he didn't say to himself, "Well, maybe Howard still doesn't like me"— Reagan would also see one of his best friends sitting on the same couch, nodding his head in agreement with Baker.

Having lunch with the Republican leadership group is probably like having lunch with the Joint Chiefs of Staff. Each member has his own constituency, a block of five to 12 members who look to them for guidance and philosophical leadership. Baker uses the luncheon to get a hold on the leaders, to gauge for himself their direction and tone and motives. These are the most powerful forces he has to deal with. He knows that sitting with him at the table today are three candidates for his position as leader when he retires: Dole, Stevens, and Lugar.

As of Monday morning, Frank Lautenberg is beginning his eighteenth week as a United States senator. Although Lautenberg is a member of the commerce committee, which is at this moment holding hearings on discrimination in the insurance industry, staff members Mary Jane Checchi and Mitchell Osteor had determined last Friday, before Lautenberg left the office, that his presence at the hearing would not be required. Lautenberg could take his time getting back to D.C. from his home in Montclair, New Jersey. Evidently, Lautenberg's staff has not been the only one to make such a decision—the hearing is attended by commerce committee chairman Robert Packwood and just two other members.

But, then, none of the other committee meetings this morning is exactly standing room only. The appropriations committee, holding hearings on proposed personnel reductions in the U.S. Customs Service, has only three members present. At the armed services committee, where the Supreme

Allied Commander for Europe, General Bernard Rogers, is testifying at a hearing on FY84 Department of Defense budget authorizations, there are more reporters in attendance than members. The finance, foreign relations, and energy committee hearings are virtually unattended as nomination hearings are concluded. This is the essence of Monday mornings in the Senate.

By missing the commerce committee hearing, Lautenberg and his aides have made for themselves a typically quiet Monday morning. Mary Jane Checchi believes this is important. It will give Lautenberg time to focus on the legislative matters at hand, and get briefed on the Central America and budget issues he will have to deal with this week. Checchi's beliefs carry a great deal of weight in the Lautenberg office. Lautenberg the novice is renting Checchi's Senate expertise while he gets his legislative feet on the ground.

Upon returning to his temporary quarters in the Russell Senate Office Building, after making a speech before the members of the visiting Cleveland Jewish Federation (as a favor to his colleague from Ohio, Howard Metzenbaum), Lautenberg sits down with Checchi and the rest of his legislative team to review policy decisions. Checchi uses the occasion to give the rookie a minilesson on the budget process, since Lautenberg will soon be confronted with the first budget votes of his short senatorial career.

While Checchi tutors her pupil in the Russell building, over in the new Hart Senate office building, Christopher Dodd's staff is preparing itself for the busy days ahead.

Chris Dodd's father, Thomas, was a well-respected member of the Senate for 12 years, until 1967, when the bottom fell out. Censured for personal use of campaign funds, his reputation was shattered and the family name was left to be redeemed by his son. In 1974, young Dodd was elected to the House of Representatives, and in 1980, against the Reagan tide, defeated former New York Senator James Buckley to become Connecticut's junior senator.

Attractive and ambitious, Dodd learned to use his charismatic speaking skills and youthful enthusiasm to attack Reagan administration policies. He emerged, very quickly, as one of the leaders of the Senate's New Left. Yet Dodd was also known as a poor manager of his time, and his attempts to be out front on a variety of issues made some of his colleagues wary of his overall effectiveness.

Tomorrow afternoon, the Senate will sit in secret session because of Chris Dodd's request. And on Wednesday night, Dodd is to deliver the official Democratic response to President Reagan's speech on Central America.

Dodd has felt for some time that Central America would be the vehicle that would bring him to the national spotlight. The combination of his work in Central America, his numerous recent visits to the region, his fluency in Spanish, and the apparent vacuum in the Senate for someone willing to take on the administration, helped him garner a position of influence that in his father's days would have taken decades to achieve.

Like many Senate schemes, the secret session plan began not in a member's head, but in the mind of a staffer. Dodd's legislative assistant for foreign affairs is Robert Dockerty, who has been on the Senate staff since 1969, when he worked on the foreign relations committee for then chairman William Fulbright, Democrat of Arkansas.

Angered by the ease with which Reagan's views and policies on Central America were becoming accepted in the Senate, Dockerty had begun to lobby Dodd about the advantages of a secret session, to investigate fully what was going on down there. He wants Chris Dodd to be the one to clear the air about the administration's intentions. Dodd bought the idea, and last week Dockerty had drafted the letter, signed by Dodd, that informed his colleagues of his intention to ask for the secret session.

Technically, the letter was not required. For the Senate to go into a closed session, a member need merely stand up and request it, and then be seconded in the motion by another member. The advance warning that Dodd gave was in part a courtesy to the leadership, since such a session will alter the

Senate schedule, and in part a necessary convenience, since the chamber has to be outfitted for such an event.

At a staff meeting of the Democratic leadership in House Speaker Tip O'Neill's office on Friday, the wheels were set in motion that would carry Dodd's face to millions of American TV sets Wednesday night. Rob Lebatore, the staff director of the Democratic policy committee, Patrick Griffin, the secretary for the Senate minority, and Christopher Matthews, press secretary to O'Neill, dominated the meeting—mostly Lebatore. One of the items on the agenda was the matter of who would give the Democratic response to Reagan's upcoming address before the joint session of Congress. Lebatore lobbied for Dodd from the start, on the grounds that Dodd had been especially vocal on Central American policy, was considered a charismatic and persuasive speaker, and, perhaps most important, looked good on television.

House aides concurred because they didn't mind letting the Senate take the reins on this one. Some at the meeting thought that Dodd might deliver a speech that would be "too controversial"—that he might go too far in opposing the Reagan administration's policy and American interests in the region. Lebatore dismissed these complaints. But they would come back to haunt him.

Lebatore went back to Robert Byrd, and told the Senate minority leader that the leadership meeting had selected Dodd to deliver the speech. Lebatore then called Robert Dockerty to tell him that Byrd would call Dodd over the weekend to invite him formally. Lebatore also told Dockerty that Dodd's staff people should not be the ones to announce this to the press; Byrd would, as befitted his leadership position.

By 3:00 P.M., the population of senators present on the Hill has grown measurably. Afternoons in the Senate tend to drag on, especially on Mondays. The bulk of committee business is done in the morning and, on most days, the major preoccupation of the afternoon is trying to get the Senate closed down for the day.

In Baker's conference room after the leadership lunch,

Range and Bell prepare strategies for getting the budget resolution passed. A few minutes before, Range had given Baker a list of senators he should talk to in the next few days, to probe their views on the budget. Baker sits in his private office as his secretary attempts to reach the people on the list. Not surprisingly, Baker finds that most of those he wants to talk to are still back home, delaying the return to Washington as long as possible.

At 6:30, Baker arrives at the Key Bridge Marriott Hotel to participate in one of the regularly scheduled government seminars sponsored by the Arthur Anderson accounting firm, one of the "Big Eight" in the country. It likes to send its executives to Washington to mingle with politicos and get a reading on Washington's economic plans. Baker will not accept any money for tonight's performance; he is there as a favor to his accountant, who works for Anderson. Baker's talk, on the prospects for passing a budget resolution, lasts about 15 minutes, after which he answers questions until 7:00 P.M. Wilbur Walker, his driver, is waiting in front of the hotel, and when he sees Baker emerge, he starts the big Lincoln's engine and turns on the headlights. Soon he and the majority leader are gliding off toward home.

2

⁂

TUESDAY

I hear senators saying on the Senate floor all the time: "My staff says that's a bad amendment." I say to them, "Yeah, well, Senator, don't you have any thoughts about it? Is that all you know about it, that your staff doesn't like it?" I've seen senators, whose character and intelligence I know reasonably well, vote a certain way just because staff tells them to.

DALE BUMPERS (D–ARK.)

They are an army of baby-boomers this legion of Senate staffers who file into the Russell Senate Office Building throughout the morning; they are factory laborers with briefcases, marching to work in a mining town that produces mostly paper, staffers dressed for success. Women lift their navy blue and black pumps out of canvas bags to replace the sneakers worn in for the commute. Dressed predominantly in prim frocks, preppy skirt-and-blouse combinations, a few even dare to wear pants, though always properly topped with snappy blazers or conservative suit jackets. Most of the men have sought the shelter of pinstripe suits or conservative sportcoats and slacks. On Capitol Hill, one doesn't shrink from such stereotypes, one rushes to join them. Disruptive individuality in choices of attire is not encouraged; the dress code is unwritten, but quite rigorously obeyed.

Upstairs, in the office of Senator Frank Lautenberg, Mary Jane Checchi is hewing to standards in a navy blue suit over a crisp white blouse. In person as well as on paper, she gives the impression of being spotlessly correct.

Checchi is a Senate veteran, and Lautenberg, the newcomer, is glad to be able to benefit from her services. Checchi graduated from Vassar, magna cum laude, and then went to the University of Chicago Law School. During her second year of law school she married, but was divorced two years later, something she would later consider one of the few palpable failures of her orderly life. Her first stint on the Hill was as a summer intern for Senator Joe Tydings of Maryland after her sophomore year of college and then during summers through law school. Her plans to continue in that job after law school were disrupted when Tydings lost his 1970 bid for reelection.

She rebounded with Ed Muskie, working in the Washington office of his 1972 presidential campaign, leaving that to pursue a writing career—a cherished dream that didn't pan out—returning to the beckoning Hill in 1975 to handle appropriations committee work for Birch Bayh, Democrat of Indiana. Things took off for her from there. In 1976 she became deputy counsel to the budget committee, and the following year joined Robert Byrd's staff as his counsel on the judiciary committee, the first woman to be hired for that position. In 1978 she became the first woman and, at 32, the youngest person ever to be named staff director and counsel of the Democratic policy committee, the Byrd-powered vehicle that set the agenda and ran the party caucuses for the Democratic majority.

Once again, however, Checchi felt the urge to write, and once again she left the Hill in search of creative fulfillment, which is difficult to find in Congress, taking a whack at the Great American Novel. This time the muse lured her all the way to France but—she returned to the Hill again, in 1982, just before Frank Lautenberg was elected as the new senator from New Jersey.

Three months into his term, Lautenberg had filled most of his staff assignments; but he still wanted someone with a widescreen perspective during the break-in period, and that coincided with Checchi's desire for an interim job only. Her task was to help Lautenberg get off to the best start he could. She started working with his legislative team on the agenda for his first year, giving Lautenberg helpful minitutorials on Senate procedure.

This morning, Checchi has been drafted into the service of the banking committee, because the position of legislative assistant for that committee's work has yet to be filled. Lautenberg and his legislative director Eve Lubalin realized after two months of interviews with job applicants that the position would be tough to fill. Anybody who has the kind of background and expertise to handle banking issues for the senator would probably already be gainfully employed "downtown"—in the more lucrative private sector—working for a law firm, or for one of the banking lobbies, and making a lot more money than Lautenberg was willing to pay, or rather that the Senate staff pay cap permitted him to pay. The problem is common. Almost all senators have been faced with the difficulty of finding new staff members or trying to hold on to those they have. Once the lobbying groups become aware of the staffers who are most skilled and savvy, they stage talent raids designed to lure them to a better paying, and often less frustrating, job. Marty Gold, an expert on parliamentary procedure who had been counsel to the majority leader, loved working in the Senate and idolized Howard Baker. But he couldn't afford to stay. He reluctantly left his job in 1982 to become a vice president at Robert Gray and Company, one of the city's biggest public relations and lobbying firms. By doing so, he immediately realized a $25,000 annual increase in salary; six months later, it was a $40,000 increase. The best people working on the Hill aren't necessarily Hill employees, but those who know how the Hill operates and who are getting paid handsomely to put that knowledge to work as lob-byists.

As 9:30 and a banking committee hearing approach, Chec-chi pulls together some briefing materials for Lautenberg. The hearings today are a continuation of oversight discussions on the condition of the domestic financial services industry, its present dilemmas and its future prospects. Three weeks ago, in the first installment, Treasury Secretary Donald Regan had appeared before the committee, discussing bank holding com-pany deregulation and regulatory reform. Oversight hearings provide members with the opportunity to remind those off the Hill that it is Congress that is the overseer of federal pro-grams and operations—not agencies, not departments. These reminders take the form of program performance evaluation, efficiency and effectiveness monitoring, administrative assess-ments, and financial priority reviews. Today's hearings will be a free-for-all on the state of the financial services industry, af-fording staff and members the opportunity to vent concerns expressed back home and from key pressure groups.

Checchi prepares two briefing notebooks, one for herself and one for her senator. Lautenberg's copy is draped by a cover memo that identifies the substantive issues he will face in the hearings, and a list of the opposing forces and players, from lobbyists to White House officials. The cast is a big one: banking deregulation has been one of the most heavily lob-bied issues before the Congress, a clash between securities in-dustries, insurance companies, and the banking community itself.

Those who testify before a Senate committee are urged to submit their prepared statements in advance whenever possi-ble; for this morning's session, Checchi has tried to track down any available statements before she turns the briefing book over to Lautenberg for the last time. She has gone through those that she has managed to retrieve to highlight what she considers to be the most important points.

Because Lautenberg is new to this game, it is difficult for Checchi to decide on an appropriate line of questioning for him. Senators who have been around for a while have established track records of what's important to them, politically or philosophically, and aides can take it from there. At first, upon his arrival in the Senate, Lautenberg didn't know which direction he should take, but he did know he was interested in getting involved in the hearing process and not being just an observer. Although Lautenberg has no legislative background, he does have a background in business—he co-founded Automatic Data Processing Inc.—and that gives him an inherent interest in financial affairs.

As a member of the banking committee, Lautenberg will be hearing testimony this morning from, and tossing questions at, Federal Reserve Chairman Paul Volcker, whose appearance will dramatically alter the tone and character of the committee and the hearings by making both, for today, conspicuously televisable. The cameras rarely show up for anything so potentially dull and august as a session of the banking committee. But with Volcker at the witness table, it is another matter altogether (although one TV reporter, believing that Volcker's newsworthiness had been overestimated, has declared he will measure the importance of the hearing by the number of cigars the Fed chairman smokes; if he has more than two, the formula goes, he's staying to make news).

Consequently, this is a day when Lautenberg needs to be seen on the committee much more than the committee actually needs him; this is true of other senators as well. The combination of Volcker and the TV news cameras inspires unusually high attendance on the committee, whose members normally show up only haphazardly. Senators, in fact, count on their legislative assistants to let their scheduling secretaries know when such stars as Volcker, and such adornments as TV cameras, will appear, so they can ask questions that will serve their interests back home, and, they hope, get themselves on the evening news. Network, if possible. A senator serves many masters. Television is one of them.

Senator Jake Garn of Utah, the chairman, opens the meeting with a welcome for Volcker, who in turn praises the committee for holding the hearings in the first place and then reads from a prepared text, a gray philosophical dissertation about technological and economic forces affecting the interaction between financial, legal, and regulatory operations. This will not be on the evening news. Lautenberg listens, sporadically taking notes. As the member with least seniority, he is supposed to ask his questions last, but since today he is one of the few to have arrived at the hearing on time, he gets to go ahead of several more senior members, who have been characteristically tardy.

Checchi sits behind Lautenberg, as most staffers do at hearings, and takes notes of her own. Lautenberg's opening question has to do with the role of technology in public banking, not necessarily a particular concern of his New Jersey constituents, but one that permits him, in one of his first major hearings on the committee, to operate from familiar ground. Lautenberg uses some of the questions Checchi has prepared for him, and ad libs others of his own, some of them arising from his interests in banking and business. At one point Volcker remarks that an insurance company in New Jersey also owns an investment house. Lautenberg cracks, "They also own New Jersey." Checchi and nearly everybody else in the room breaks into laughter. "Not really," Lautenberg quickly adds—for the record.

The two major committees that Lautenberg was assigned to when he came to the Senate—banking, housing, and urban affairs, and commerce, science, and transportation—enable him to be involved heavily in transportation issues in addition to telecommunication matters. Both are very big games, as played in New Jersey. The banking, housing, and urban affairs jurisdiction also translates well both in terms of his business background and for the problems of his state. For the rest of his senatorial career, barring a committee transfer, Lautenberg will be regarded, by virtue of his assignment, as an expert on these issues. He will be asked to speak on the subjects at conventions.

In the mornings, most of the Senate's business is done in

committee; in fact, most of the Senate's work is always done in committees. The committee has largely replaced the floor debate as the arena for legislative change. Senators are conspicuous joiners when it comes to committees. They're supposed to join only two major committees and one minor committee, but the system encourages them to garner as many assignments as they can. William Armstrong, Republican from Colorado, says that the ability to vote by proxy enables a senator to overextend himself with committee positions. "The way the Senate is set up," Armstrong says, "it rewards a member who gets involved in everything, even though he or she may not be a very active participant. By being a member you get a certain leverage on a lot of deals, in a lot of different ways. So, even though it's impossible really to participate in three committees, four committees, ten subcommittees— whatever it is—if your interest is in affecting the outcome of legislation, there's an incentive to be on every committee you can get on."

The Volcker show is not the only committee performance going on this morning. At hearings of the labor and human resources committee, opera star Beverly Sills and Dallas Cowboy Drew Pearson testify as part of committee efforts in behalf of health care and disease prevention. Labor staffers had booked the glamorous pair over a month earlier, and their appearances today not only brought in the TV cameras—as it was planned they would—but gave the room the ambiance of a Phil Donahue show. Bringing in Hollywood and sports figures is fairly common committee procedure. The stars generally can count on being stroked by the chairmen and all the members. Who would be mean to Beverly Sills?

Both the armed services and governmental affairs committees are wrestling with the latest device for circumnavigating political quagmires—the bipartisan commission. At the armed services subcommittee on strategic and theater nuclear forces, members are resuming consideration of the strategic modernization program (a.k.a., the MX mess), which was endorsed by the Scowcroft Commission at the beginning of the month. The subcommittee is hearing from General Bennie Davis, commander-in-chief, Strategic Air Command, and McGeorge Bundy, former national security advisor.

The governmental affairs committee is in the process of reporting out a bill calling for a new Hoover Commission. The Hoover Commission, named for its first chairman, Herbert, was established by statute in 1947, then again in 1953, as a vehicle for the legislature to study the organization of the Executive Branch. The new commission not only would replace the latest one—which preoccupied itself with members' pay—but would also be charged with no less a task than to "improve the quality of government in the United States" and "restoring public confidence in government at all levels." Seasoned Senate veterans who have had a gander at this mandate take it as a certain sign that this whole bipartisan commission business is getting out of hand.

"Surrogate mayors" is one way to describe the job of members of the D.C. subcommittee on appropriations, and this morning they are doing their best to penetrate the labyrinth of the district bureaucracy. Meanwhile, the energy and natural resources committee is still attempting to mark up natural gas deregulation measures, but its chairman, James McClure, is caught between White House indecision, natural gas interests, and Democratic resistance. And so it goes.

Just before 8:30, Howard Baker's car pulls up outside the entrance to the Capitol Hill Club on 2nd and D streets SE, disgorging the majority leader. The club is a Republican watering hole—for breakfast, lunch, and dinner gatherings at which corporations can hear members and GOP officials preach the party line. Huge flattering portraits of Baker and House Republican leader Bob Michel greet visitors at the front entrance and give them a pretty good fix on the political persuasion of the management. With Republican Reagan in the White House, and Republicans outnumbering Democrats in the Senate, only an influx of Republicans into the House, enough to make Michel the Speaker, could make them happier.

Baker is here to rattle off a few remarks to the American Cookware Manufacturers, who are happy to get him, and happy to pay for getting him. In Senate circles, such an event is known as The $2,000 Quickie, since that is the limit a senator can earn for a speech. It's a bargain for the corporations, which would have to pay nonelected speakers of significant stature anywhere from $5,000 to $10,000 for an appearance. For the members, the cap may be $2,000 per speech, but at present there is no overall annual cap on such earnings—although every year some troublemaker proposes that there should be. Some of the higher profile members have started to make big bucks off these honorariums by hopping over to nearby hotels and clubs with great frequency—and considerable enthusiasm. In 1982, Baker made over $50,000 from speeches but was still short of the Senate's honorary honorarium champ, Senator Robert Dole of Kansas. He brought in over $90,000. Dole likes to leave 'em laughing. Usually, he himself exits smiling.

Last night, personal secretary Triplett placed a manila envelope describing today's speech in Baker's briefcase. Driver Wilbur Walker got his own envelope, with the same prompting sheet, as well—a safety measure made necessary by the fact that Baker habitually misplaces things, like envelopes with speeches in them. Since press secretary Tommy Griscom makes most of the decisions on Baker's speaking schedule—Baker occasionally reminds him that he wants more honorariums—the majority leader rarely knows more than a day in advance where he will be speaking. The envelope from Triplett also contains a photostat of the original invitation, a guest list (with the names of guests from Tennessee underlined), and a set of talking points.

Baker is at his best when expounding off the cuff. He feels uncomfortable with prepared texts when he is in front of audiences; he likes to keep his head up to comb the group and make as much eye contact as possible. The crib sheet gives Baker an outline of specific points and the general theme of the talk. Usually, there are one or two pages of three-sentence messages which Baker digests in the car on the way to a speech. If he likes what he reads, he will bring the copy up to the podium, weaving into the written text the trademark southernisms, Dirksen anecdotes, and other standbys he relies on to keep an audience hooked.

Today's talking points focus on the budget; along with the growing interest in Central America, the budget is the biggest ongoing story in the country. Baker hews to the theme, holding forth for 14 minutes about the mess the deliberations have become, after which he tells the audience that he is due at the weekly leadership meeting at the White House, but he will be pleased as punch to answer their questions. At 9:00, Baker sees a nod from the staff person accompanying him (he is never alone), apologizes to the audience, and bolts through the side door.

Baker climbs into the car and greets Walker with a "Hello, Wilbur!" so hearty it's as if they have been separated for months, rather than the 25 minutes it has taken Baker to make his $2,000. Walker tells Baker that his secretary has called to say they have to stop at the Capitol for a changing of the guard—the staff member who has accompanied Baker to the cookware bash is to be replaced by Griscom, whose job will be to run interference with the press at the White House.

Since the beginning of his presidency, Ronald Reagan has played host on most Tuesdays to Baker, majority whip Ted Stevens, Reagan pal Paul Laxalt, House minority leader Bob Michel, and House minority whip Trent Lott of Mississippi. White House chief of staff James A. Baker III and congressional liaison director Ken Duberstein operate from the president's side. For Senator Baker, the meetings have afforded an opportunity to watch the president make decisions, see what his dispositions are toward Congress, and, when possible, influence White House strategies. The relationship has gone better than most at both sides of the avenue ever thought it would.

When Reagan was elected in 1980, it remained to be seen how much the measures that Congress had adopted during the seventies to curb the "imperial presidency" had deprived any president of the ability to lead; how determined the new breed of congressman was to frustrate any presidential leadership; and to what degree this burgeoning incapacity was the result of Jimmy Carter's personal ineffectiveness.

Ronald Reagan was determined to restore presidential leadership to a relationship in which it had often seemed stubbornly stagnant. He wanted to be the de facto leader of Congress, the leader of the nation, and of course the leader of the Free World. He believed a mandate had been bestowed upon him. Through television, he would cement this mandate; in the House and Senate chambers he would execute it. Reagan was also convinced that the public wanted his leadership, after a period of exasperation with both the presidency and the Congress.

In September 1979, Jimmy Carter's approval rating in an Associated Press poll was 19 percent, the lowest level of any presidency on record. But the public approval rating of Congress had somehow managed to do even worse—13 percent, or 30 percent below Carter. It was safe for Reagan to believe his relationship with Capitol Hill would depend much more on his personal attributes than on the elusive character of Congress. Thus the Reagan era began with the eagerness and dreamy passion that often mark political commencements; a nice way to start off a honeymoon, particularly with a newly elected Republican majority in the Senate.

Reagan began his presidency doing what presidents do best, and what congresses do worst—looking at the big picture. It was a decision reached even before the election, for it fit into his political dynamic; as many members of Congress would soon learn, Reagan was more disposed to respond to themes and crusades than to details and entanglements. Such a posture, it was thought, would give Congress something to follow while at the same time leaving members free to attend to their parochial interests. The real task for Reagan was to convert rhetoric into implementation.

Not since Lyndon Johnson had a president granted so much importance to his relationship with Congress. Although Eisenhower had made congressional affairs somewhat more visible, and Kennedy had increased the staff responsible for them, Johnson, particularly early on, developed the office of congressional relations—the most convenient caretaker of Congress—to previously unattempted (and largely undesired) heights. Johnson's experience as majority leader, his zeal for persuading, and his determination to prevail, made him a likely meddler in congressional intricacies. Here was a president who, the story goes, read the *Congressional Record* every morning in his bedroom; one who not merely participated in the business of the office of congressional affairs—granting senior members of the staff free access to the Oval Office and setting up direct lines to them in turn—but in effect actually dominated Office of Congressional Relations proceedings.

The Congress LBJ left just a few years earlier had changed to such an extent, however, that relations between the Hill and the White House were now much more complex. A decline in party discipline and in the influence of the "Whales"—the powers to be reckoned with—created the need for more staff to gather intelligence for the president on what Congress was up to, and how Congress would act. The burgeoning role for the congressional relations staff coincided with a diminishing role for the traditional power structure in the Congress. This general condition was due in part to Senate majority leader Mike Mansfield's egalitarian brand of leadership and his frustration with many Johnson policies. The Mansfield staff even began to make it a habit not to share its vote counts with the OCR staff in the White House. Reagan, still mindful that congressional victories for his team would strengthen public support, made the legislative affairs operation a major element in White House operations.

As the car rolls down Pennsylvania Avenue, over bumps and into potholes, Baker again takes note of the raggedy state of the road, which seems to him to be undergoing perpetual repair. The endless construction and destruction of one of America's best-known thoroughfares once prompted him to speculate, in remarks on the Senate floor, that crews were simply digging up one side of the street, fixing it, doing the same to the other side, and then starting all over again. His comments elicited a written response from the director of the Pennsylvania Avenue redevelopment project, who said he was sorry Baker was miffed and offered him a tour of the construction, which, the director claimed, was ahead of schedule. Baker sent a staffer.

White House guards signal Baker's car through the northwest gate of the White House; Wilbur Walker moves it slowly up the curved driveway to the entrance, where a flock of reporters swoops down on it, hoping for comment and being put off by Baker until after the meeting. Griscom stays outside with the press, and the majority leader walks into the White House; he is saluted as he enters by the marine guard on duty. As soon as he gets inside, Baker sees Steve Bell bending the ear of Senator Domenici. Bell talks fast, because although Domenici will be at the meeting, Bell will not. He tells the budget committee chairman—Reagan's recent phone call to Domenici is on both Bell's mind and Domenici's—to hold firm and wait for more compromises from the White House.

While the 1980 elections altered virtually every national political career, few in the Senate changed to the same degree as that of an immigrant Italian grocer's son, Pietro Vichi Domenici. Since 1981, he has been one of a few individuals at the very center of the budget firestorm. For eight years since his election to the Senate in 1972, Pete Domenici served as an unassuming and nationally anonymous spokesman for New Mexico interests, seemingly content with bargaining as a junior, minority member of the environment and public works and energy and natural resources committees.

A chain smoker who worries incessantly and shleps around meetings with his trouser cuffs dragging on the ground, Domenici has been suspected by some to breathe budget numbers instead of oxygen. He is likeable, genuine, and principled, a proudly ardent supporter of the budget process.

As one of the budget's most important caretakers, Domenici oversees analysis of billions and billions of federal budget dollars even while as a private citizen he struggles to keep his family financially secure and his eight children in school. Domenici's committee is one of the most visible on the Hill. Its proceedings customarily make news, and for good reasons: the budget committee's impact on the president's programs, its effect on other committees, and its significance to the financial markets are obvious.

As the committee's staff director, Bell has more influence over the man he calls "Boss" and over what Bell calls "my" committee than any other staff director in the Senate. Bell's squatty but muscular frame suggests a large brick with arms and legs; if you bump into him, chances are you will be the only one to notice it. For roughly nine months out of every year, he is partial to wearing a fluorescent striped suit that makes him look like an ice cream salesman.

Bell likes to play political hardball, exhibiting endless enthusiasm for the infighting and struggles that are a large part of his job. His behavior is beyond type A: aggressive, nervous, shrewd, unrelenting, and exceedingly authoritative. He controls a committee that has a majority staff of close to 60 staffers, and even Bell admits that he has developed "a very hierarchical system." Everything goes through him: parking assignments, vacations, raises, firings, and hirings. A memo Bell wrote to his staff after a sparsely attended meeting reflects his not-so-subtle management philosophy: "Obviously I could go to the extreme of docking the salaries 10 percent of those people who were late or did not attend the staff meeting this morning. However, I would prefer not to do that. But failure to be on time or attend staff meetings indicates a disinterest [*sic*] in the workings of the committee and it might be that you would prefer to find more interesting work elsewhere. I await written notification of your decision to attend staff meetings, and attend them on time, or not to work here. The choice is yours."

Baker has called Bell "one of the most powerful staffers I

have ever met," high praise from a Republican, especially considering the fact that Bell had supported Eugène McCarthy for president in 1968.

Bell was married when he was 17 and a half ("that's what happens in west Texas when you get someone pregnant") and received undergraduate and graduate degrees in English. His master's thesis was on the poetry of Robert Frost. He was working in the Public Information Office of the University of New Mexico when he was asked by a Domenici operative if he wanted to be press secretary during Domenici's campaign for the Senate in 1972.

The first time Domenici met him, Bell was wearing a T-shirt, big mutton chops, and very long hair. Domenici wasn't too impressed. Not until five weeks later, when Domenici ridiculed his appearance, did Bell change his act to short hair and three-piece suits. Domenici thought Bell abrasive and alien. But he liked the guy, no doubt about it. And he valued Bell's advice over practically everyone else's.

Although this is the president's meeting, today the president will not be there. The meeting this morning will be with White House chief of staff Jim Baker. The reason is that the budget discussions this morning are considered too specific and too strategic to take up the president's time.

Senator Baker begins the meeting by painting a picture of the divisions within Senate Republicans, and follows with a breakdown of the major camps. Jim Baker listens and zeros in on two concerns: first, whether the president is facing a potential political defeat, and second, which members might possibly be influenced by a call from or meeting with Reagan himself to prevent such a catastrophe.

In a sense, the meeting could serve as a snapshot of Howard Baker's political life since 1981, embodying its two most important elements: his (and Congress's) relationship with the White House, and Republican efforts to control the budget and the budget process.

Throughout the preceding two years, the Baker and Baker

team has been through a variety of ups and downs with the budget, but both are aware that the episode they are now embarked on could prove to be the most aggravating of all. The partisan elan that had launched them on their merry way is now long gone. The way looks less merry.

The screenplay for the battle of the budget in Reagan's first term was conceived on Sunday, January 4, 1981, when the new powers-to-be gathered at Howard Baker's Washington home to focus their attention on the launching of the new administration. The idea was originally that of Reagan pollster Dick Wirthlin, but it was James Cannon, Baker's chief of staff, exercising cautious judgment and political prudence, who felt it looked wrong symbolically for a pollster to convene the team's first important powwow. So it became Howard Baker's show.

Baker used money from his own political action committee to pay for the dinner, which may in part explain why the meeting started off with just one drink for each guest, followed by a quick walk-through buffet. Then came the discussion.

It was the first large meeting after the election victory, and once word got around that it was going to be an important meeting, everybody, particularly those who were embroiled in fighting for key positions, wanted to attend. The positioning for power would prove to be as entertaining as the policy discussions themselves.

Baker's guest list included his fiscal chairmen—Dole of finance, Hatfield of appropriations, Domenici of budget, Garn of banking, and Laxalt of Reaganville. From the president-elect team came Jim Baker, Ed Meese, Don Regan, David Stockman, Alan Greenspan, David Gergen, Marty Anderson, and Wirthlin. It was Wirthlin who kicked off the meeting with a presentation of what it was that Ronald Reagan was ostensibly elected to do, why Americans voted for him, and what they expected of him now.

Senator Baker then gave his own pitch. He said that whatever was decided he felt that the key to implementation was moving as quickly as possible—there was no guarantee as to how long a honeymoon would last. That got nods and grunts of agreement all around, but Baker wasn't so lucky with his next brainstorm—the suggestion that, in his State of the Union address, the president declare that, after looking things over, he had discovered economic conditions were worse than he thought and that the country should accept a moratorium for 90 days on increases in cost-of-living adjustments, contract negotiations, everything. It was Baker's modification on wage and price controls.

Baker said the president should use his "raw prestige" to make this bold move, which would in turn give him more opportunity to work on his own budget proposals. But after he finished his presentation, Baker got what he later describes as "a lot of flak." Don Regan was one of those attending who believed that economic conditions weren't all that serious; Meese grumbled that such extreme actions were not consistent with Reagan's character. Baker retreated on this point, as he would on many others in the years to come.

After the Baker idea was shot down, Wirthlin discussed the social agenda—school prayer, busing, and abortion. Here Baker was more successful. He proclaimed that he did not want to fight every economic bill with social legislation attached—that the economy should be the first priority and that social issues should be debated afterward. This made sense to those attending, or so it seemed, but no one had any guarantee that the New Right, which felt that the Republican party's big election victories were tied in with the social issues, would agree.

It was budget director Stockman who brainstormed "reconciliation" as the framework for the dramatic fiscal realignment in 1981. "We wanted something big and new and rolling fast, to break down parochial resistance," Stockman would say later. He knew the Democratic House was not the place to launch this offensive; the Senate, with its new Republican majority, was a more ideal venue. When Stockman first shared his plans for reconciliation procedures with Howard Baker, the majority leader was not yet aware of the potential clout of the maneuver.

After 1981, reconciliation became the most important word in the fiscal lexicon. It was deployed that year in an unprecedented degree, bringing smiles to the faces of those who embellished its meaning and frowns to those who had included it as part of the 1974 budget act. For the Republican majority in the Senate, and the White House, reconciliation was a commodious vehicle that enabled the new president's economic programs to move quickly and boldly—one great effort to adhere to the promises of the 1980 campaign.

Several characteristics distinguished the reconciliation instructions of 1981 from those of any previous year. First, the instructions covered a three-year period—reflecting the multiyear perspective of Reagan's program and his desire to lock in major changes in federal policy, and reflecting Bell's and Domenici's determination to strengthen budgetary control. Second, the process was more sweeping in its scope, applying to many more committees—15 in the House and 13 in the Senate. The budget committee had become King of the Hill. Third, some committees were directed to cut authorizations as well as entitlements. Authorizations, unlike entitlements and appropriations, do not establish financial commitments; instead, they are the substantive laws which create programs and establish the policies governing their operation. Authorizations may set overall constraints on the amount and purpose of funding, but funds are provided separately in annual appropriation acts. In this case, the Reagan administration hoped to secure reductions in future appropriations by restructuring the authorization laws governing certain programs.

When President Reagan signed both the massive reconciliation and tax cut bills at his Santa Barbara ranch on a foggy day in August of 1981, the Reagan romance with the Republican Senate was in full bloom.

Just one month later, however, the administration sent to Congress a revised budget requesting additional spending reductions. That package, containing approximately $12 billion more in domestic spending cuts, never made it to either floor of Congress. The reductions had started to hit the middle class, and the severity of the spending cuts was beginning to hurt Republicans, who were gearing up for the 1982 election, just a year away. Thus did the once-idyllic affair between Reagan and the Senate Republicans begin to sour. Would they love him in the coming year as they had in July? Not if they saw that as a threat to their own political fates and fortunes. When all's well, when the president's policies are popular, senators attach themselves to him for all to see; when things aren't so rosy, senators suddenly become more independent. It's the survival instinct at work.

Not surprisingly, then, formulation of a budget in 1982 proved to be a more difficult and prolonged exercise. The president submitted a fiscal year 1983 budget on February 8, 1982; it sparked a forest fire of criticism—the prevailing sentiment in Congress being that the president's recommendations made unnecessarily deep cuts in domestic spending and provided defense spending with too great an increase, while leaving the deficit at the unacceptably high level of nearly $92 billion.

Recognizing that the original budget submission could not muster adequate support in Congress, Baker organized a series of meetings with representatives from his camp, from the president's, and from Speaker O'Neill's. The informal negotiations lasted only several weeks; the group came to be known, by its size, as the Gang of 17. They were unable to forge a compromise on the politically explosive social security issue, and, when it became obvious that no agreement was in sight, Baker asked the president if he himself would be willing to negotiate.

The president agreed to the plan, and told Baker that he would invite the Speaker to the White House. Baker told both the president and Jim Baker that he thought that it would be a more politic and symbolic gesture if the president came to the Hill for the meeting. The gathering, with the president, Howard Baker, O'Neill, majority leader Jim Wright, and whip Ted Stevens took place behind the Senate chamber in the Capitol.

When Baker walked into the gathering he was so struck by the uniqueness of the situation that he asked an aide to run back to his office and retrieve his camera. After Baker finished taking his snapshots of history (the only ones of the day, since the press was not allowed into the meeting), the doors were closed. O'Neill took a deep breath and proceeded to lambaste the president about the unfairness of his economic policies, and proclaimed his own unwillingness to be any part of them.

The president was patient during this tirade, just listening—though several later noted that while the Speaker was leaning toward him for emphasis the president's cheeks turned even redder than usual. When O'Neill finished, Reagan went back at the Speaker with the same fervor. Baker remarked later that it was like "two heavyweights" going at each other. With such a rancorous start, it was no surprise that no agreement came out of the meeting.

Senate deliberations on the budget resolution were not much easier. They were nearly stalled at the outset: on May 6, the budget committee favorably reported the budget resolution by only a two-vote margin, 12 to 10. The vote was split along party lines and presaged further partisan wrangling on the floor. The measure passed the Senate a few weeks later by the fairly narrow margin of 49 to 43.

The House and Senate came into final agreement on the first budget resolution on June 23—about six weeks past the deadline prescribed in the budget act, though most were happy to get anything. In order to avoid resurrecting these difficult issues in the fall (just before elections), Baker and Domenici took up the crowd-pleasing tack of providing for an automatic second budget resolution—to become effective on October 1, the start of the fiscal year. As it had not done in 1981, the Senate found its own voice in 1982, at least on budgetary matters.

The Senate has found its own voice in 1983, too, and that's what chief of staff Jim Baker is worried about at today's meeting. Domenici's refusal to acquiesce to the president on defense spending during their recent phone call, and the budget committee's decision to pass a budget the White House deplores, are still fresh in the minds of both Jim Baker and Howard Baker as the morning meeting wears on. Domenici is following Bell's whispered advice to hang tough for more compromises, to the displeasure of Jim Baker. The meeting, which lasts nearly an hour, proves as a result to be another of this week's exercises in futility.

When Baker returns from the White House, he is met in the conference room by Range and Cannon. Baker sits at the head of the table, the signal that a meeting or get-together of some sort is about to occur. Range is laughing about an article in the morning *Washington Post* concerning Senator Roger Jepsen of Iowa, who on the previous Friday morning was traveling in the high-occupancy vehicle lane of route 395 and was stopped by a police officer for being alone in his car; the law requires four occupants during rush hour. Ever resourceful, Jepsen invoked congressional immunity to avoid the $35 fine; when he'd told the policewoman who stopped him that he was a senator and constitutionally immune, she just tottered back to her car and drove off.

It is only 11:00 in the morning, but Baker already looks tired. He has budget on the brain, and he isn't disposed to start thinking much about anything else. Range realizes it, and begins a series of questions aimed at figuring out what had just gone on at the White House.

Range has more access to his boss, and is involved with more legislative dealings with his boss, than almost any other staffer in the Senate. Baker highly values the roles Range plays in deliberations: monitoring other staff work; devising strategies in cooperation with Howard Greene, the secretary for the majority, in the cloakroom; and acting on Baker's behalf at the countless meetings and inquiries he is too busy to attend. To do all these things, Range spends much of his day listening to and trying to figure out what Baker wants; the rest of the day is given over to talking, grabbing, and pleading with those who are in a position to help him get there.

In Cannon's view, Range, in his tireless drive to ascertain what went on at one of the few meetings he didn't attend, is getting too aggressive and asking too many questions. So Cannon goes into his specialty act: making expressions and hand gestures out of Baker's sight that signal the need for a cooling down. Range gets the message and, though it is against his nature, relents. For now. Baker tells Range that the meeting with Jim Baker didn't hold any surprises anyway.

"Simpson," Range tells Baker, "is getting his act together and will be able to roll on Thursday." Immigration is exactly the kind of thorny problem Baker feels he doesn't need this week.

Eleven-thirty is the appointed hour for the weekly meeting of all the Senate committee chairmen, and Baker is on hand, as is his custom, to receive the chairmen as they wander into the conference room. The meetings are attended by the 18 chairmen of the standing Senate committees, the ubiquitous Senator Laxalt, and sometimes Vice President Bush. Baker also invites one freshman and one sophomore to each meeting. Today, Mack Mattingly of Georgia and Rudy Boschwitz of Minnesota are the chosen ones. Baker has been holding these meetings since before the Republicans won control of the Senate—a kind of shadow Senate leadership that would allow the Republicans to begin to learn what they should do when their time came, as Baker felt it soon would.

Domenici is the first to arrive, eager as usual and spouting off to Baker aides the problems he foresees ensuing on the budget in the next few weeks. Like a shadow, Bell escorts Domenici into the room, though he knows he will not be allowed to stay for the meeting. Range, who will stay—always stays—has prepared an agenda for Baker, as he does every week. Today, Baker will discuss the closed session of the Senate that will take place a few hours later; the bankruptcy bill;

and the immigration bill. But Range has predicted in his proposed agenda that most of the discussion this morning will be centered on what to do about the budget resolution slated for the following week.

The meeting opens with Garn and Packwood expressing their displeasure at the fact that the prolonged July recess has gone by the wayside. Baker insists that he simply can't let people go what with the appropriations bills pending, and that the Speaker and Jamie Whitten, chairman of the House appropriations committee, had promised to send the bills over before July.

McClure, as chairman of the Republican conference, says he has received a request for a Republican caucus on the budget, a formal gathering in which participants would try to formulate a unified plan. Only Range and Baker are paying close enough attention to notice that McClure hasn't said *who* has requested this conference. Range interprets this to be a ploy by McClure to take the budget battle into his, and the conservatives', back yard—the Republican caucus—instead of letting Baker control it. Baker politely says that looking for a party position right now would be extremely difficult since sharp divisions exist; a caucus could prohibit his ability to get a majority of the Republican members together on some of the more important issues by placing them against a wall. Range recognizes another reason behind McClure's call for a conference: Baker's announced retirement has not only diminished his ability to manage and influence other members, it has also set the stage for the battle to succeed him as majority leader.

No one wants to talk about the budget any more, and so everyone is relieved to see Al Simpson signaling for the floor, even though he has a look on his face that seems to say, *I hate to bring this up, but.* It is no mystery what he is bringing up: the immigration bill he is cosponsoring and wants to see action on this week. Simpson, a sardonic pragmatist, has had plenty of experience with senatorial exasperation: "I happen to chair three things—veterans affairs, nuclear regulation, and immigration—all three sons of bitches are just filled with guilt, fear, emotionalism, and racism or in some way a mixture of one of those four," he says. "But then you find yourself as a reasonable person who does his homework having to fend off people who just grab a microphone and get everybody all juiced up, which is very easy to do in this town.

Skeptical but seasoned, Simpson now hopes he can move the immigration bill through quickly, another of those false hopes that grow like daisies on the Hill. But he is also smart enough to know that neither he nor Baker can really control deliberations on the bill. The immigration issue cuts across so many lines—political, regional, philosophical—that even Simpson, who has been immersed in the bill for the past two years, cannot predict its fate.

To his credit, John Tower of Texas, who is famous for opposing immigration reform because—as he has often been quoted as saying—"90 percent of those people coming across the border are going to register Democratic," has decided against obstructing the bill, fortunately for Simpson, at least for the time being. Watching as Simpson attempted to put his immigration package together, Tower has remarked on more than one occasion about the skillfulness and resourcefulness that Simpson had exhibited. Baker breathes a deep sigh of relief when Tower says it again at this meeting, even though Tower had earlier privately told Baker he does not intend to fight against Simpson's bill to the bitter end.

There are many elements to Simpson's bill, but the explosive rubric under which all of them line up is really a battle among Hispanic, agricultural and labor interests—a battle fought perpetually, and never to a decision, in Congress, and so hard to settle in any one piece of legislation. But Simpson has bravely taken on the role of referee, and knows that he is making enemies on this, as he would no matter what he did. Growers want something from him, unions want something from him, the Hispanic Commission wants something from him, and of course the government wants something else again.

Around the Senate, Simpson is the member least likely to be accused of taking himself too seriously. He is considered by those who work with him to be a bundle of laughs—or, more accurately, a towering stalk of laughs, since he stands 6 feet 7 inches tall, weights only about 180 pounds, and is rarely without a good, or at least a well-intentioned, joke.

Simpson's father, Milward, served in the Senate from 1946 to 1953 but didn't come close to making the impact that his son has made since his election in 1978: Simpson père visited his son in the Senate one day in 1979 and left the place muttering about how much things had changed along "the aisle." He was deploring the shade of gray that had replaced the old black-and-white adversarial relationship between Democrats and Republicans. Indeed, his own son later made headlines with a vituperative, slashing attack on Jesse Helms during the 1982 lame duck session. Helms had launched a filibuster that threatened the other senators' Christmas vacations. Simpson, looming over Helms in the Senate chamber, exploded, "Seldom have I seen in my legislative experience of 17 years or more, a more obdurate and obnoxious performance. I guess it's called hardball. In my neck of the woods we call it stickball. Children play it.

"It seems the whole issue of the senator's tenure as I have observed it in my short term seems to be 'How is it playing in North Carolina as to peanuts, tobacco, and family farm?'"

The chamber was hushed. Simpson had spoken for many. His attack on Helms also dramatized the fact that the old game was being played by new rules.

Now it is Domenici's turn to speak at the chairmen's meeting. He tells his fellow chairmen that the House is sure to use its budget targets in the appropriations process if the Senate doesn't act quickly on the budget resolution. He spells out for the other chairmen, for the first time since the resolution was reported from his committee, the strategy he wants to follow. Levels of domestic spending could not go any lower without seriously jeopardizing chances of passage, Domenici says. While conceding that revenue levels will have to be raised, Domenici says that, unlike the Democrats, he thinks that should be put off as long as possible. He concludes by saying Republicans need to convince the White House of these realities.

Hatfield reacts to Domenici's revenue strategy with skepticism, worrying aloud that the Democrats will be able to turn to the Republicans and accuse the GOP of favoring those dreaded big deficits. This pretty much ends the meeting. Baker leaves the chairmen the way he has found them: without consensus, without direction. Twenty or even ten years ago, chairmen were older, more clearly products of the institution, and able to decide amongst themselves the course the Senate would take. Today's chairmen are comparatively powerless and much less capable of steering the Senate.

In room S-211 of the Capitol, as the antique clocks are striking noon, Senator Chris Dodd is sitting down with his Democratic colleagues for the weekly Democratic luncheon. He knows that they know he is about to complicate their lives. In two hours, he will formally ask the Senate to take the extraordinary step of meeting in closed session.

He feels his colleagues looking at him with something less than rapt admiration. Some of them clearly do not appreciate this gesture. They think it is unnecessary and bothersome. Dodd is already worried that he may be doing the wrong thing at the wrong time. But it is time to play the game for real, and he tries to exude the utmost confidence in the decision he—and his staff—have reached. It is his face, of course, and not his staff's, that is hanging as a target should this entire gambit go awry, as gambits on the Hill are wont to do. But he knows he has to banish such self-doubts now that the ball is in his court.

Minority leader Robert Byrd has other things on his mind. He is keenly aware of the importance of keeping the Democrats in line on the budget. This is his mission for the week, and this is the line he is pitching at the Democrats' anchor.

Byrd has, in the minds of many Democrats, actually become a more effective leader since losing the majority leadership; he seems to be concentrating more on working with all members to make sure their concerns are vented, rather then preoccupying himself with the management of the Senate floor as he did in the days when Mary Jane Checchi was working for him in the majority leader's office.

Floor leaders' roles as party spokesmen to the public have often changed. Dirksen excelled in that role like a happy tout at a convivial racetrack; Mansfield and Byrd were criticized for not pursuing it. There is potential conflict, both in institutional and in personal terms, between finding someone who makes the trains run on time and someone who looks good on the evening news. Byrd has long known what Byrd does best, and doesn't appear to mind that his skills are not the type of which galvanic national careers are made.

The man who is Baker's Democratic counterpart clearly has his charms, and they are old-world charms sometimes lost on new Senate upstarts. On quiet afternoons, for instance, Byrd is fond of presenting, even to a largely empty chamber, personal "history lessons" on the Senate. He stands motionless behind his front row desk, often in a red plaid vest, his borderline bluish hair combed in opposite directions from his forehead until it meets again in the back. Then, pedantically—some would say—he traces the developments behind the Missouri Compromise or the issues discussed in the Webster–Hayne debates, quoting from memory passages from speeches and poems that annotate the past with creativity and humor.

In encounters with colleagues, both publicly and privately, Byrd is a willing, avid listener, yet many find him a difficult person to talk with. Conversations tend to be short and utilitarian. Professionally, Byrd is a study in resolve and rigidity, but privately his friends say that, emotionally, he has never been the same since his grandson was killed in a traffic accident in 1982. It jolted him into a new awareness, some believe, that there is more to life than life in the Senate.

After Byrd finishes his unity pitch on the budget at the luncheon, he turns the floor over to Lawton Chiles, the rank-

85

ing Democrat on the budget committee, who brings his colleagues up to speed on the budget resolution. He once again pleads for their cooperation.

When John Tower looks up and sees Howard Baker striding into S-207, he knows it is the signal to convene today's Republican policy luncheon, a weekly sociopolitical event that comes cheap but not free. By tradition, each member attending has dutifully anted up $5 for the modest meal to be served. Part of the lore of these affairs (and on the Hill, if there is an affair, there is sure to be lore to go with it) is the story of how President Reagan, invited (upon his request) to attend one of the luncheons in 1981 for the purpose of special pitching, learned from his staff about the customary $5 fee, and offered to pay it to Howard Greene, who as secretary for the majority is in charge of making the collection. Greene said that he couldn't take money from the president. Reagan insisted he was just one of the boys and wanted to pay his own way. So Greene took one of his own bills and put it into the pot for Reagan. He then asked the president to sign the $5 bill Reagan had intended to contribute and reimburse him. That autographed bill was later framed, and is spending the rest of its life hung on a wall in Greene's office.

The Tuesday meetings, something of an institution, are really the only scheduled time that Senate Republicans get together as a group, on their own, during the week. This Tuesday's meeting will prove to be absolutely typical of the breed: there are innumerable problems waiting to be solved; a unified and solid party stance has to be formulated on each of them, and, as almost invariably happens, none will be. Even though they are all Republicans, 54 people with their own individual ambitions are not about to suppress them over tiny salads and rare roast beef. In this sense, the luncheon is a microcosm of the whole system and its foibles.

Baker begins his comments by expressing his gratitude for the messages of concern he received while he was at the hospital over the weekend (and anyone who had neglected to send such a message got a picture in his mind of which staffer to blame for that) and repeats to the group what he has told most of them individually, that there is nothing seriously wrong with him, no ulcer, not to worry.

Then he has a less innocuous matter to bring up. He reminds the luncheoneers that, as per the request of Chris Dodd, there will be a closed session of the Senate, for the purpose of considering the situation in Central America, in one hour. The session will probably last 90 minutes, Baker guesses, and intelligence committee chairman Goldwater will control the time allotted to Republicans. There is a smattering of muffled groans. Most members consider this "secret session" a waste of their time.

Now, about the budget. Baker says that he hopes to move to the budget resolution as soon as it is available, but warns his fellow Republicans not to expect too much Democratic assistance when the budget finally comes up. In the give-and-take that competes with the clattering of plates and silverware as the meeting continues, Republican conference chairman James McClure announces that he wants to schedule a conference meeting for Wednesday at noon, if it is all right with Domenici. Domenici says that will be perfectly all right; Tower allows as how early Thursday would be better for him, but is defeated in that motion by a show of hands in favor of Wednesday. Tower concedes on that one, and concludes by reminding everyone at the meeting about the importance of acting quickly on the resolution and the importance of maintaining a cohesive Republican position.

A cohesive Republican position? From the start of this latest budget adventure Baker has felt that is too much to ask, or to hope for, and he lets Tower know that. There are just too many pieces to the budget to expect such a miracle, Baker tells him. And then he voices a rather unrealistic expectation of his own: would all those present please not blab anything to the press until after tomorrow's caucus? Baker knows it is an almost foolish hope, but he makes the request just the same. You never know; somebody might actually take it seriously.

The discussion now turns to the perpetually tantalizing

topic of extending the summer recess so that senators will have two full months off, instead of the planned one month. Baker has to repeat the sad tidings that the Speaker and Jamie Whitten, House appropriations chairman, have promised that most of the appropriations bill will be sent to the Senate before July; with all that work sitting in the Senate's lap, the possibility of extending the recess looks slim. This is the really bad news communicated at the luncheon. It is enough to curdle nondairy coffee creamer.

Baker's discouraging announcement is a hard act to follow, but judiciary chairman Thurmond steps gamely in to give a quick briefing on the bankruptcy bill, since it is expected that the bill will be hitting the floor on Wednesday.

The nagging subject of the secret session returns. Malcolm Wallop of Wyoming says he is confused about where Republicans should stand on the Central America situation, and says he has become even more mixed up since calling the White House that morning and receiving no real help, although Bush had told him to work with Senator Goldwater and remember the president's position. Tower, Baker, Wallop, and Mattingly bat the issue around for a while. Wallop says he fears Dodd will charge that the administration is not complying with the law, and that Senator Daniel Patrick Moynihan of New York will say that, although the administration is obeying the law, it is sloppily giving the public the impression that it is not. Baker steps in to plead yet again with members not to say anything to the press about the session; Tower seconds that and then some, speaking in stronger terms than Baker has used and reminding his colleagues that any member who reveals what happens in a closed session is subject to the discipline of the Senate.

Mark Andrews of North Dakota says he thinks the administration isn't helping its own case on the Central America question. Mattingly says that what the Republicans in the Senate need is a spokesman, and Tower reminds him that Goldwater is it. Nancy Kassebaum of Kansas says she feels there is too little, or no, cooperation from the White House.

Dave Durenberger of Minnesota says that members can receive information through the intelligence committee, and that the less said before the president's speech the better.

Mattingly has a sorrowful tale for his colleagues to ponder. He says that the week before he had called the National Security Council for information about the country's Central America policy; whoever had answered the phone asked him what state he was from, and what party he belonged to, but never called back with any information. They didn't seem to know who he was. A couple of the members at the meeting use their napkins to hide chuckles at Mattingly's indignant recollection. Howard Baker is not so much chuckling as imagining that happy day when he won't have to attend meetings like this and listen to soliloquies like that any more.

As the discussion lurches on, Warren Rudman of New Hampshire asks whether senators should even attend the secret session and Richard Lugar of Indiana says yes, absolutely they should—but that he isn't sure whether he will be able to make it or not. Baker suggests that everybody should be there, regardless of how they feel about the idea of having a secret session in the first place.

John Chafee of Rhode Island and William Cohen of Maine chime in next, Chafee saying the session is deplorable on the face of it and Cohen stating, quite astutely, that there is nothing to be learned in a secret session that senators couldn't read for themselves in the *New York Times*. The Central America issue boils down to two questions, Cohen says: is the administration complying with the law, and can the law even be complied with?

Oh, and by the way, Cohen adds—souvenir jackets for the Republican National Convention are now on sale. After that announcement, Strom Thurmond asks that any senators who aren't using their tickets to the joint session of Congress, at which the president is speaking tomorrow night, give them to him so he can distribute them to the wives of cabinet officers. There being no objection, and pressing matters like souvenir jackets and joint-session tickets having been settled—if no others—Tower adjourns the meeting at 1:45.

The Democrats and Republicans aren't the only ones having luncheons today. Over in the Russell building, the Senate Wives Club is holding a ceremonial lunch in honor of First Lady Nancy Reagan. At the head table with her are Joy Baker (in a wheelchair from a knee operation), Erma Byrd, Helen Jackson, Collene Nunn, Cathy Stevens, Barbara Bush, and Carol Laxalt. The women present the First Lady with a sign inscribed "First Lady's Park," to be installed at the First Couple's much cherished Santa Barbara ranch.

At 2:00, Baker convenes the Senate, stating that a request for a closed session, to begin at 2:30, is anticipated. Privately, he is still hoping that Dodd has changed his mind. Privately and publicly, Dodd is considering no such move.

The logistical wheels for the closed session are already well in motion. For several hours now, a team of technicians under the direction of sergeant at arms Howard Liebengood has been preparing the chamber. In the morning, all floor personnel were asked to leave and the chamber doors were sealed. Then, debugging exterminators moved in and "swept" the chamber and the galleries to make sure no recording devices were present. All phones in and around the chamber were disconnected, and monitoring equipment was set up to make sure no recording devices were smuggled in after the chamber had been swept. Liebengood also had the rather unpleasant and certainly unpopular duty of clearing out the press room. Reporters bitched loudly as they were hustled out, but since the press room opens onto the press gallery above the Senate floor, it too had to be emptied.

At 2:06, Baker moves that the Senate stand in recess until 2:30, to give senators a chance to come to the chamber for the secret session. At 2:33, Dodd moves that the Senate doors be closed. Paul Tsongas seconds it. This is it. Second thoughts are worthless now.

Once the session had been scheduled, Dodd and his staff found themselves in a somewhat awkward position. Since neither Dodd nor Tsongas is a member of the intelligence committee, neither really has anything to say; they want to hear, to be information receivers rather than givers. Yet they are the ones who have started it.

Secret sessions are handled by the select committee on intelligence, which is responsible for monitoring sensitive and classified information. There are 15 senators on the committee—eight Republicans, seven Democrats—assisted by 15 staff members, all of whom have top secret code word clearance. This includes secretaries and clerks, who must be cleared by the FBI. Each senator on the committee can nominate one person to represent his interests and assist him. Most staff members on the committee are ex-CIA employees, military, or ex–foreign service personnel. In its current composition, the staff even includes a couple of academics. The committee is designed to be a consensus committee, and under Goldwater and Moynihan it has steered away from advocacy and moved toward being a source of information.

When Dodd's request first surfaced, most of the intelligence committee grumbled and groused. Some felt Dodd was out to embarrass the committee and the administration and that nothing would come of the session. Others felt that the session would actually work against Dodd's interests since information would emerge to calm the fears of many members who'd been caught up in the media campaign against the administration's policies.

Some people are merely angry about the session, but Barry Goldwater is furious. He had offered to take Dodd over to the intelligence committee's office and let him read any and all classified documents about Central America. But Dodd declined, holding to his insistence on the more noticeable closed session. Though Goldwater cannot stop the session, he knows he can at least try to manage it, and does his best.

Goldwater grouchily begins the session with a terse opening statement, outlining the parameters of the discussion to follow. Dodd then gives a spirited defense of his reasons for requesting the session. Then Moynihan offers a capsule description of the general Central America policy of the United States.

Attendance at the session is high at the beginning—this is a thorny issue, after all, and the president will be speaking about it Wednesday night at the joint session—but senators begin to drift out of the chamber even during the session's first half hour. Howard Baker believes that these sessions have more genuine give-and-take than do nonsecret ones, because the press isn't there, and most members are past trying to impress each other. Members also talk free of the constraints of official Senate procedure, which can sometimes be awkward and anachronistic. Such rules as "When a senator desires to speak, he shall rise and address the presiding officer, and shall not proceed until he is recognized," are jettisoned for these occasions. But Baker's enthusiasm is not shared by many others.

What most of those who stayed will remember about this secret session is the dressing down Texas Democrat Lloyd Bentsen gives his younger colleague Dodd. Bentsen, normally calm and stately and not given to vituperation, becomes forceful and emphatic when he warns Dodd against ignoring the dangers to American security posed by developments in Central America. Baker, leaning back in his chair at the front of the chamber, thinks to himself that Bentsen's remarks are some of the most impressive he has yet to hear on the subject.

Later, Goldwater would grumble: "This session would have never been allowed 20 years ago. Those freshmen senators would have been called in the back room and they would have been reminded that you don't use your own preferences, even though it's within the rules, to upset the daily work of 98 other senators."

For Goldwater, this is another example of how Senate decorum is eroding and how the new generation of senators are making mincemeat of the traditions set down by the old. "I served with Dodd's father and I have tremendous respect for his father," Goldwater says. "I think one of Chris's main troubles is that he's trying to live up to his old man and he can't do it. And the evidence is that the two men who called for the session made utter fools of themselves with the information they thought they had."

The session may be secret, but the fact that it is occurring is not; the announcement was made at the beginning of the week, it was widely publicized, members' staff were duly informed, and only an hour earlier it had been discussed in the party caucuses. However, one senator has still managed to be blithely unaware that the session is occurring. As it starts, Frank Lautenberg is in the Russell building, chatting away obliviously. It's not that Lautenberg had planned to miss the first secret session of his senatorial life; rather, there had been a little mixup at the staff level—the kind that occurs innumerable times each day and the kind that can be extremely embarrassing to the member.

Mary Jane Checchi is now chagrined that even she, the Senate pro, has failed to deliver Lautenberg into his seat on the chamber floor in time for the secret session. Senators do not have to be responsible for being in the right place at the right time; that's the staff's worry. Some senators are moved around by their staff like chess pieces. Checchi is embarrassed, but not particularly guilt-ridden; she knows it wasn't her fault, nor even the fault of any one particular person. It was System Breakdown at work.

Lautenberg, as he is forever reminding his staff, loves to take advantage of every minute in the office. He is often among the last members to arrive for votes, because he waits until he absolutely has to go. Lautenberg's staff had asked the Democratic cloakroom to call the office as the secret session was about to get under way. But the cloakroom assistants, busy with other things, and mindful of the fact that they had earlier told Lautenberg's office the session would start at 2:30, didn't make the final confirmation phone call. Lautenberg's forgetful staff had let him jabber on about the broadcast industry with some ABC radio and television executives, even as the doors of the Senate chamber were being closed and tempers on the floor were just beginning to flare.

As it happens, the meeting is important for both Lautenberg and his guests. Because Lautenberg is now a member of the commerce committee, which oversees regulation of the broadcast industry, Lautenberg will automatically be a popular fellow with the broadcasters. The broadcasting lobby is considered by some to be the most powerful on the Hill. It has roughly the equivalent of All the Money in the World to throw around. And it just loves to throw it.

The ABC boys want to meet Lautenberg so they can size him up; will he be a softie and a pushover, or will he be trouble? Broadcasters can largely dictate to the FCC how much regulation they will tolerate, but sometimes senators and representatives can monkey-wrench the works. The meeting with Lautenberg is jolly, but so lengthy that it costs Lautenberg the chance to attend his first secret session of the Senate. In retrospect, however—after he realizes what he missed—Lautenberg knows it might well prove to have been worth it.

A secret session can lead to a public relations dilemma: what is to be done with the information once it is obtained? If nothing is reported to the press and the public as a result of the session, then the whole thing looks like it may have been wholesale grandstanding. If the session produces some sort of incendiary hot potato, one is placed in the awkward position of releasing classified information. Even if you are lucky enough to find out something, you are damned if you say and damned if you don't say.

The next morning, the *Washington Post* will give the secret session only passing mention—noting it was "unusual"—within a larger story about Central American appropriations.

A long day of haggling over Central American and budget problems has come to an end, and Baker has escaped to the apartment of his friend Bob Healy, to dine with a group that includes syndicated columnist Jules Witcover, top-flight reporter Al Hunt of the *Wall Street Journal,* and other journalists. It is the type of get-together that Baker loves, because it gives him the opportunity to chat off the record with reporters. Reporters, for their part, love almost nothing more than off-the-record chats, and Baker is one of the ablest chatterers on the Hill.

Thanks to Hunt, the conversation gets around to Baker and his reaction to a statement Paul Laxalt made to reporters that morning: he had instructed "restless" supporters of the president to "cool it" until the president had decided if indeed he intended to run for another term.

Baker's first response to Hunt's question is a forced smile. Deep inside, even he doesn't know what the president has decided. Deep inside he wants like hell to know, because very deep inside, Howard Baker naturally wants to be president himself.

3

WEDNESDAY

The first six months it's how did I get here, the next six
months it's how did they get here. You get frustrated some-
times. Some people really drive you up the wall. They're never
with you and they're always finding fault. You get a little
tired, and I think you get spread too thin. Someday you're
going to get your feet chopped off too, because you're meddling
around in so many different things—but there's a vacuum
out there.

ROBERT DOLE (R-KANS.)

Alone in the Capitol rotunda, so early that neither workers nor tourists have yet stormed the Hill for another day, one
can stroll and contemplate, even ponder. Heroic statues stand
silent, turbulent patriotic tableaux hang from the walls. High
above, concave within the dome itself, looms Constantine
Brumidi's "The Apotheosis of George Washington," which
treats the first president approximately the way Michelangelo
treated God. The Goddess of Liberty and the Goddess of
Wisdom in fact share the fresco with Washington, and with
Benjamin Franklin, Robert Fulton, Samuel F. B. Morse, and a

semiheavenly host of others, 180 feet above the rotunda floor.

At this hushed hour, with the orchestrated chaos of the day yet to commence, it can be cathartic, even inspiring, to stand here alone, with history. One or two hours from now, when the daily bedlam has resumed, many of those who work in this building and the others on the Hill will begin to feel pessimistic, cynical, even hopeless. They will be lost in major and minor bickerings, struggles, and scenarios. But now, within the huge rotunda, the aura is entirely different. It's mind-clearing. Watching for ghosts, listening for echoes, one really might sense the presence of the elusive but abiding belief that unites all these people and links them to what is still, two centuries later, an imposing ideal. This can be a spiritual place.

But not for long. By 8:30, there is already too much bustle to allow for reverence. Today will be a more hectic day on the Hill than most. The president of the United States is coming to the Capitol tonight to speak to a joint session of Congress on his hotly criticized Central American policy. Some of the newer Republican members, excited over the drama of the president's visit, have even been predicting that the speech will be a critical turning point for the Central America issue.

Howard Baker knows better. In the past, he has watched the Congress respond to such initiatives by grinding them into bureaucratic dust; he can do nothing now but hope that this one will turn out differently.

Neither the impending visit nor the disputed policy, however, is the topic of conversation excitedly going on among the women who work in Baker's office. Huddled in colloquy, gesturing and sputtering, they couldn't care less about the president at this moment. "He'd better not," someone warns from within the group, and another groans, "Oh, I would just *die!*" What they are just dying over is National Secretaries Week, which had started Monday, and rumors that Baker plans to deliver a speech on the Senate floor this morning praising his "secretaries" and, even worse from their point of view, naming names.

The women much prefer not being named by Baker on the Senate floor; to them, this is not even remotely an honor. In Baker's office, as in others on the Hill, executive assistants do not like being called secretaries; staff assistants do not like being called secretaries; even secretaries do not like being called secretaries. Emily Reynolds, who carries the title executive assistant to the chief of staff, is particularly miffed. With Baker's imminent retirement already announced, she has been looking ahead to a much bigger and better line of work.

Baker's speechwriter, charged with the duty of composing the remarks—and threatened by several of the women if he follows orders and includes their names—is in a bind. He can't go to Baker and tell the leader he has all but engendered a palace revolt with such a simple thing as this; Baker doesn't thrive on that kind of news, and is, as usual, grappling now with larger issues. A mere trifle in retrospect (such retrospect as is achieved merely an hour or two later), the issue at the moment seems traumatizingly crucial.

Meanwhile, the morning leadership meeting is actually beginning on time, though on a note even less serious than that sounded by National Secretaries Week: all those at the meeting are still chortling about the way Senator Roger Jepsen had used congressional privilege to wiggle out of a traffic ticket. After about five minutes of this, Baker shifts gears: he says he will tell Robert Byrd, the minority leader, that the Senate will be in recess from 12 to 2 today because of the Republican conference on the budget. "This is a double-barrel high-risk day," he says, and most people understand what he means: that the prospect of a party caucus on a budget the press knows to be in trouble because of dissension in the Republican ranks, combined with the fact that the president will be waving his potentially divisive Central America policy around like a flag later that evening on the Hill, has the potential to spark public relations fires Baker doesn't have the time or, in some cases, the influence to extinguish.

The key to solving the difficulties, Baker knows, will be to work them out far from the prying ears of the press. His mission for the day will be to attempt to convince his colleagues not to run to reporters after the caucus, even if no agreement is reached; Baker is convinced that this would only damage whatever chances for agreement remain. Toward this end, Griscom, the ever-vigilant press secretary, is now told to be as visible as possible with Hill reporters today. Griscom has a reputation for carrying around in his head things reporters think they need, and he has calculated that if he can give them enough inside information about how things will turn out, they won't go digging elsewhere.

Range will spend the morning monitoring key players' staffs for insights into what Baker may be confronted with at the noon caucus. It's the kind of espionage assignment he loves, and invariably pulls off with earthy panache. He already knows he will devote most of his attention to Bell, who has been throwing the staff of Domenici's budget committee into a tizzy, not to mention several of the members themselves.

Range and Greene report to those at the meeting that they have devised a short-term schedule which calls for the budget resolution to come up on the floor the following Monday. Baker asks if this has been checked out with Domenici. Range says yes, he has mentioned it to Bell, and Bell has given it his okay. That is good enough for Baker; Bell is so solidly established as a budget player that his signoff is as good as Domenici's.

But over at the budget committee offices, the trust is not returned. Bell has gathered the senior staff from within his empire of more than 60 assistants, and is now reaffirming his determination to pass a resolution next week, even if it isn't one that the president and the majority leader want.

Since he became a staff director of the budget committee, Bell has never experienced such tension in his committee and in the complicated budget process as surrounds him now. His aims, both for what he sees as the country's economic well-being, and for Domenici's political survival, stand in direct contrast to the expressed will of the leaders of the party. But Bell's instructions to his analysts remain firm: he wants a bipartisan plan that will raise revenues, cut defense increases, and give his boss the credit for reducing the deficit. For perhaps the hundredth time, Bell says, "Weinberger made us look like idiots" during mark-up, and "I ain't going through that again."

Bell is still waiting for his chairman to give him the go-ahead to take on the big boys (Reagan and the majority leader). He has already drafted the speech in his mind: "I'm sorry, Mr. Leader, but I'm leading the fight against you. We carried a lot of water for the man downtown in '81 and '82, and we were lucky that we kept the majority after the close elections. But what you've given me is an impossible task."

At 10:01 A.M., Richard Halverson, the chaplain of the Senate, utters a prayer from the front of the chamber as the Senate officially opens for the day. The prayer has been a long-standing and noncontroversial custom. Will Rogers took note of it when he cracked, "About all I can say for the United States Senate is that it opens with a prayer and closes with an investigation." Halverson is customarily reverent this morning. "As Congress anticipates its joint session and the president prepares to address it on exceedingly vital issues, may he be given special wisdom and may the people be attentive and responsive," he intones. "May Thy will be done in America as it is in heaven."

Praying done, president pro tempore Thurmond recognizes the majority leader in accordance with Senate procedure, and Baker, smiling, begins his remarks by saying how "fascinated" he is by the chaplain's prayers. Baker likes Halverson; he doubts that anyone would be capable of not liking this amiably gregarious fellow who walks around shaking hands with staffers on the Senate floor once his prayer duties are over and telling each of them, "God bless you, brother." The one common criticism of him is that his opening prayers are often too long. Sometimes staffers make mad dashes for the cloakrooms when the bells ring to signal the start of the session. They can talk in the cloakrooms while the prayer is going on (and on) and don't have to bow their heads in silence. Once, during a really long prayer, majority secretary Greene peered through the window of the Republican cloakroom and said that he was going to file a cloture motion against Halverson if he didn't shut up.

After complimenting the chaplain, Baker's next order of business is also on the metaphysical side. In honor of Shakespeare's birthday the preceding Saturday, Baker announces, he is substituting five of Shakespeare's sonnets for "the traditional weekly poem." The weekly poem doesn't go back very far in Senate tradition. About a year earlier, on a Friday afternoon, Baker had asked his speechwriter for something "different" with which to begin the following Monday's session. He found a poem on his desk when the day arrived, and when he balked at the prospect of reading a poem on the Senate floor, he was told he didn't have to read it aloud, he just had to insert it into the record. Henceforth, Baker would be known as the majority leader who opened each week of the Senate with poetry. The southern romantic within Howard Baker's practical soul liked that.

Other senators and members of their staffs, presumably charmed by the idea, began submitting poems for Baker's consideration (Teddy Kennedy once forwarded one submitted by a constituent); then the press began to notice the practice and found it endearing. Baker thought maybe it was getting out of hand, however, when poetry groups started sending in requests that he come and recite to them. He was comfortable with the idea of inserting the poem into the record, but not with reciting one, on the Senate floor or anywhere else. Usually black dots are placed in the record next to statements that are not read "live" on the Senate floor, but Baker and Byrd never have dots next to their names because chief printing clerk Russell Walker believes they are too busy and too important to be saddled with dots. Maybe decades, centuries, or eons from now, historians will assume that Howard Baker stood before the Senate and recited poetry. Howard Baker would not mind if they did.

Now comes that dread item on the agenda, Baker's comments pertaining to National Secretaries Week. It has been a close one. Three minutes before Baker had entered the Senate chamber he was handed a statement. He had speed-read the three pages—he is a highly proficient speed-reader of statements he is about to make—and had asked where the names of the "secretaries" were. He was told that naming the secretaries wouldn't elicit quite the response he thought it would. Baker laughed in acquiescence. Like that, he saw the light.

The statement Baker now reads calls into question the appropriateness of the term "secretary" when applied to those who do so much more than the word suggests, who reject the stereotype of the secretary as "a nail-polishing, gum-cracking woman on the prowl for a husband, with a body-temperature IQ." Baker concludes by saying, "I want to freely confess before the Senate and all combined that the women and men who conduct the work of the world in so many staff positions are the ones who really get the work done and those of us who stand in the fore and occupy positions of responsibility in business, in industry, and in public life owe an extraordinary debt of gratitude to these individuals. It does not make any difference to me whether people want to be called secretaries or staff people, or executive or administrative assistants or anything else. I want to publicly proclaim that we could not get along without them."

Senate proceedings are piped live to the offices of members, and at their desks the women who had been agitated and worried earlier are now placated and pleased as they listen to Baker's remarks. This has been an extremely tiny squall in the overall context of male–female relations on the Hill, but it is emblematic of the changes taking place in the status of women there—changes that many feel are not only overdue, but also lag dramatically behind those that have occurred elsewhere.

Since Jeanette Rankin became the first woman elected to Congress in 1916, 110 women have served either by appointment or election—less than 1 percent of the membership since 1789. The 98th Congress has only two female senators, Republicans Nancy Kassebaum of Kansas and Paula Hawkins of Florida.

At the staff level, while women do occupy over 60 percent of the positions in the Senate, they do not wield a corresponding amount of power. In general, salaries paid to women Senate employees are less than salaries paid to men; women still hold comparatively few policy-making positions, and they are promised professional jobs less often than men are.

Jobs women hold are generally more clerical than administrative, commanding high levels of neither responsibility nor salary. Males outnumber females three to one in the Senate at salaries above $18,000. But the inequities can be glaring even within certain job categories. A 1980 study reported that the mean salary for a male Senate employee was over $24,000, while the female salary was just over a paltry $16,000. In nearly every category of job description, women make less than men. Not only are they more likely to occupy the types of jobs that pay less, but even in the same type of work, women earn less than men do.

Such disparities do not rest solely in Senate salary statistics. The level of actual responsibility of the jobs held by men and women differs. Only about 14 percent of the women on Senate staffs are in "policy-making" positions; approximately 49 percent of the men can be considered policy makers. At the start of the 97th Congress, there were also twice as many men (539) in policy positions as women (267).

Forty-one percent of all women working in Senate offices hold clerical positions, as opposed to 7.2 percent of all male employees. Over 90 percent of all executive secretarial, clerical assistant, receptionist, and secretarial positions are held by women. Men actually face discrimination when applying for such jobs; their mean salary is less than women's if they decide they want to answer phones or sit behind a typewriter.

Senators can get away with blatantly unequal employment practices because Congress has exempted itself from all the civil rights laws it has passed, including Title VII of the 1964 Civil Rights Act and the Equal Pay Act. A senator can hire, fire, and pay with no regard to any such standards. Each member of Congress individually staffs his or her own office and has no government-mandated personnel policy or salary scale to follow. This can provide an open door for an ambitious rising staff member to pursue a high salary and to exert influence—but for many Senate employees the lack of equal protection only serves to limit access to such positions.

The most effective staffers of either sex—those who earn their boss's trust and thereby manage to flourish—have to learn quickly to repress ideological positions and opinions that conflict with those of the members for whom they work. The easiest route is to have no ideology at all, or to purge oneself of whatever ideology one does have, and many follow it. Those who cannot adapt one way or the other often end up living lives of quiet, or noisy, desperation. Rare is the senator who enjoys arguing the merits of issues with his staff, formulating a stance, and then tolerating dissenting opinions from within his own ranks.

Nonetheless, the staffer is more than a bystander watching the legislative parade go by from the side of the road. He or she can become among the most constructive, or destructive, forces at work on the Hill. This is primarily a byproduct of the ongoing quest for faster and greater acclaim and influence by senators. In 1967, the total number of personal assistants to senators was 1,749; by 1980, this number had increased by two and one half times, to 4,281. The phenomenon of the burgeoning staff is also part of the fallout of the thousands of promises made to voters in campaigns to undertake more and more responsibility. And so America's ambitious youths migrate to Capitol Hill to sign on to the ever-growing employment rolls.

The Legislative Reorganization Acts of 1946 and 1970 not only facilitated larger personal and committee staffs, they authorized the amassing of vast legions of new federal employees to lend Congress assistance (and perhaps help it grow still bigger). The Congressional Research Service, the General Accounting Office, the Congressional Budget Office, and the Office of Technology Assessment—all established by the reorganization acts—are the kinds of collaborative gifts only Congress could give itself, partly to assuage the fear of ever having to rely on outsiders. As a result, Congress is now a network of 535 functioning fiefdoms—plantations where the promises made to voters are harvested and the seeds of newly acquired roles blossom into still more staff positions.

For presiding over this giant conglomerate, senators get press attention, incalculable convenience, and free expertise at their disposal. For submitting to the quirks and whims and ambitions of their bosses, staff members in turn receive semi-impressive incomes, and a role, sometimes a key role, in the formulation of government policy. But best of all, in the view of many who've passed through Senate portals on the way to higher ground, staffdom can be an important, invaluable career step.

On this Wednesday morning, Senator Chris Dodd is doing nothing more urgent than having a friendly breakfast with his new colleague from New Jersey, Frank Lautenberg; Dodd is giving Lautenberg an update on the closed session Lautenberg missed because he was hobnobbing with broadcasters. But Dodd has a lot on his mind, especially the speech he will give tonight on national television after another of the president's cunning crowd-pleasers.

It has fallen on two members of Dodd's staff, not Dodd, to write the speech. Dodd's Butch and Sundance are Bob Dockerty, the aide whose idea the secret session had been, and Mike Naylor, Dodd's chief legislative director.

Both Butch and Sundance are veterans—Dockerty since '67 and Naylor since '75—and they could write a speech with their eyes closed. But this is a big, big speech, the biggest either has ever worked on, and there will be many more collaborators contributing to it.

Dockerty has known since last Friday that the Democratic

leadership selected Dodd to deliver the answer to the president. He has taken advantage of the head start and spent the weekend working on Dodd's speech. He wanted an "educational" speech rather than the standard media rhetoric.

On Monday morning, Dockerty handed the draft to Mike Naylor. Naylor liked what he read, but he felt that the speech was more suited for the written page than for the TV camera, and lower key than what he believed Dodd wanted. Naylor spent most of Monday and Tuesday working on revisions of his own, and Dockerty also went back to make more changes. Other staffers were feeling a bit left out of this exciting new chapter in their boss's career—but once the importance of the response to the president set in, most were glad they weren't going to be held responsible. By today, Dockerty and Naylor have gone over and over the speech, and know the wisdom of saying to themselves, *Okay, stop. That's it.* Dodd, however, has been showing the speech to everyone in sight, soliciting input high and low. One of Dodd's aides jokes that Dodd is so apprehensive about the speech and so anxious for input that he is "showing it to elevator operators to get their opinions on it too." Dodd is nervous. He is worried. All right, he is scared.

But it just isn't right yet, he thinks. He had looked at the "final draft" the previous night and found it wanting. Patrick Caddell, the pollster with the polka-dotted beard, was called in to give it a once-over and decreed that a section about how the United States is supporting guerrillas in Nicaragua and fighting them in El Salvador is too confusing. It has to be simplified, even though it is felt—indeed, known for certain—that Reagan will be oversimplifying the issue in his own speech.

Dockerty and Naylor go at it again. Naylor calls his old debating partner from college, Robert Shrum, who is press secretary for Ted Kennedy and who wrote Kennedy's thrilling "the-dream-shall-never-die" speech for the 1980 Democratic National Convention, to help out. Shrum cleans up several passages.

When Dodd comes back to the office from breakfast with

Lautenberg, he is read a section of the speech that Dockerty and Naylor have just written. It includes a reference to the "ill-educated, ill-housed, ill-motivated" people who live in Central America. Dockerty and Naylor think this is "a nice rhetorical effort." Dodd has another reaction. "What the hell is this?" he barks at them. "Who are you guys writing this for—Yale graduate school?" He says, "Let's put it in some tactile terms." He wants more about mud huts, and how the people in the region "couldn't read and couldn't count." This is to be a speech from the heart. Not the head. Reagan has to be fought with Reaganesque techniques.

Dodd wants his speech to reveal the reality of life in Central America, what it is like to live there. He himself has traveled and lived there, and he believes that the White House line on Central America is at odds with what is really going on; the Reagan administration has misrepresented the issues through oversimplification. Dodd will have ten minutes to change America's mind. He wants to go in there with all guns blazing.

He is now driving the speechwriters crazy with his demands for inserts and rewrites, and yet Dockerty and Naylor will later say that they have never worked for someone whom it was so easy to say no to. Dodd accepts their advice readily, though he does save the final option for himself, and some of the language in the speech is his own. Throughout the five days they have been laboring on the speech, Dodd had worked with his crew as equals. It has been an easy environment for them.

But many of Dodd's Democratic colleagues are not so happy. After copies of drafts began to circulate—seemingly everywhere—Democrats began bombarding Dodd's office with complaints and insistence that the speech be toned down.

In the Democratic caucus yesterday, Rob Lebatore, the staff director of the Democratic policy committee (whose lobbying last Friday had been essential to Dodd's selection to give the speech), had told Dodd that he would work with Byrd and let Dodd know about some of the minority leader's concerns, ones that would be couched not so much with respect to specific policies but with regard to overall party image. Aides to Bentsen, who was upset that Dodd would be speaking for the party, would also be consulted.

But now other agitated members have also started telling Democratic aides that they are worried about the speech. So Byrd, after hearing from House majority leader Jim Wright, has suggested that Dodd should start the speech by stating, "I am not speaking for my colleagues." The Dodd office is indignant at this suggestion; it undermines Dodd's role. Naylor says that it will be fine with him, so long as the president says at the beginning of *his* speech that he isn't speaking for all Republicans. Few now know if this is a Democratic party speech, or just a Chris Dodd production.

At 10:20 A.M., Howard Baker sits down at his desk in the center of the Senate floor and reaches into a private drawer for his secret stash of Velamints. He is waiting for Byrd to finish a conversation with his scheduling staff, so he can find out what the Democrats are planning to do when he calls up the immigration bill tomorrow. Around the floor, more members are present than is usual for the morning hour. The pro forma session on Monday and the abbreviated session Tuesday have prevented members from giving their customary morning business speeches, and they are anxious to take to the floor and deliver them. These speeches are used as constituent thank-you cards, or simple senatorial notice-mes, or for the introduction of new legislation. If it's a big policy or news-making statement, members usually race upstairs immediately after making the speech and head for the television gallery, where they make the speech again, this time for the cameras. The room, or one wall of it, has been seen frequently by TV news viewers. The senators sit or stand before a backdrop consisting of a blue curtain and bound copies of the *Congressional Record*.

Today's opening speeches have as their running motif the

fact that this Wednesday marks another annual Armenian Martyrs Day. This is the kind of event that cannot go unrecognized on the Senate floor. After Baker and Byrd finish publicly discussing the Senate schedule—with Baker once again repeating his intention to move to consideration of the bankruptcy bill—Democrat Carl Levin of Michigan, with an Armenian staff member by his side, forcefully delivers a statement marking the sixtieth anniversary of Armenian genocide at the hands of the Turks, and places in the record seven articles pertaining to the subject. They will take up more than half a dozen printed pages. Members put articles or editorials into the record to supplement their own speeches and to call attention to points of view they endorse. When Levin is finished, his Michigan colleague Donald Riegle takes up the Armenian gauntlet, as well. One might deduce from all this that there is no great shortage of Armenian voters in Michigan.

After that, senators Henry Jackson of Washington, Rudy C. Boschwitz of Minnesota, and Pete Wilson of California contribute their own solemn remarks on the anniversary. In the *Congressional Record*, there will also be statements from senators Tsongas, Heinz, Pell, and Lautenberg. None of them is present on the floor during the speech-giving (Lautenberg is stuck at a banking committee hearing), but their statements will still be printed in the record so they can be duly noted by the voters back home. They will never know that the senators haven't actually made these remarks aloud—not unless they can translate the little black dot that appears next to each absent senator's name.

At this moment, Range and Bell are plotting budget strategy in Range's office; Griscom is in the press gallery feeding information to reporters; and Mary Jane Checchi is at her rightful place behind Lautenberg at the banking committee hearing. They and nearly 7,000 other Senate staffers dutifully tend little plots of legislative earth in the name of their masters.

Among the 20-or-so job titles in a Senate office, the range

of responsibilities varies greatly. The title with the most consistent profile from office to office is the administrative assistant (AA), who serves as the member's top aide and who supervises the political, personal, legislative, and financial operations. AAs generally have logged strong records of association with their bosses—colleagues from private law practice, campaigning, or simply long-time friends. Closeness and trust are paramount between the AA and the member; an AA makes decisions for a senator hundreds of times a day. Most AAs enjoy the benefits of having their own secretaries, and in the 97th Congress earn more than $50,000 a year.

The legislative director, who makes between $25,000 and $45,000, customarily is a lawyer, and usually is in charge of coordinating the affairs of the legislative team, which includes the legislative assistants and legislative correspondents. Because most aspire to a major role in formulating and moving legislation, legislative directors tend to find the managerial facets of their jobs limiting; and as a result, many legislative directors also take responsibility for specialized areas, like environmental issues or health policy matters. Legislative assistant is the most popular and coveted position, since there are usually several in each office, all of them theoretically responsible for most issue-related work. Some LAs earn as little as $20,000 a year while others are in the high 40s.

Legislative correspondents usually spring full-blown out of college; they're highly qualified and ambitious, but not experienced enough to perform instantly the duties of an LA. Correspondents spend their days answering constituent mail with the help of constituent-minded computers that are programmed with responses to all possible kinds of inquiries. Some members even have computers that sign their names for them.

The press secretary, in most offices joined by a press assistant (some have four or five of them), is of course in charge of arranging press appearances and writing press releases; but this is a position that varies radically from staff to staff. In some offices, like Baker's, the press secretary travels with the senator and becomes companion, close advisor, and hand-holder. In others, press secretaries do little more than carry the boss's ashtray. In recent years, the chain of command has usually put the AA between the press secretary and the senator. As a result, one network correspondent says, there are only "six or seven" press secretaries in the Senate who know what their bosses are really thinking, and who are therefore worth being buttonholed by reporters.

Many a member has been known to argue that the most important, and perhaps most powerful, staff position in Senate offices is the personal secretary, sometimes referred to as executive assistant, almost always a woman. Required to deploy a combination of toughness and congeniality, personal secretaries are like those who look after presidents or chief executive officers in the private sector—their hours are long, they get involved in various personal business matters for the boss, and they tend to be the person relied on most. But on the Hill, the secretary must in addition coordinate the activities of the senator and keep colleagues on the staff apprised of his whereabouts.

There are many other staff positions—clerical assistants, staff assistants, research assistants, project assistants, assistant assistant (not an official title)—those whose duties range from acting as liaison between state and Hill offices to working for the legislative team or assisting in secretarial chores. Most offices now have computer operators who manage and attend to the keypunch, automatic pens, and mass mailing machines.

Almost all those taking these positions get caught in a common Capitol Hill limbo: they may be overqualified, but they are also underexperienced. They spring out of college, degrees in hand, hoping for a policy-making position right off, but what they find open to them are less desirable jobs, many of which can be dead ends or tickets to real or imagined oblivion. They may spend their first months, then their first years, answering phones, opening mail, or writing replies to constituent letters (those the computers can't handle) in an attempt to build a base from which to advance. There are no guarantees that they will. Starting as a secretary can mean ending as a secretary. If you do a good job, you're typecast as a good secretary, not someone with the potential to be a good senior staffer. Others take entry-level jobs in the hopes of bringing in rent money while "looking around" for something better. But it's tough to look around for another job on the Hill when you're already working there. If a job in another office comes up, and you go for it, then that office calls your current employer for a recommendation. Your current employer discerns you are dissatisfied and resents it. One's future may begin to fall apart before one's weary, bleary eyes.

After three months of operation, Lautenberg's office staff has largely solidified, although one of its pivotal members, Checchi, is technically a temporary employee. Lautenberg thinks of Checchi as the avatar of professionalism and expedient efficiency. She's held so many jobs on the Hill that she qualifies for the title of Old Pro.

When Lautenberg got to Washington, key aides made him aware of the fact that the staff that had helped him through the campaign and proven itself invaluable was now in fact largely expendable. The right people for a campaign can be the wrong people for a Senate office. Of the 70 who worked on Lautenberg's campaign, 50 applied for the 55 positions available in Lautenberg's office. Only a handful got them. Instead, the call went out around the Hill that Lautenberg was looking for a few good persons. More than 3,500 resumes had been received after the election victory, and soon the little transition office set up in the Dirksen building was engulfed in so many additional applications that it was hard to open the door for the glut of papers stuffed under it.

In part, this boom in available manpower could be traced to the great Democratic crash of 1980. Suddenly there were 12 Senate staffs, with more than 750 employees, out of jobs; newly elected Democrat Jeff Bingaman of New Mexico and Lautenberg provided a chance for many former Senate staffers to return.

Many of those hired by the new Lautenberg staff had "connections" of one kind or another. His new legislative director, Eve Baum, had worked for Birch Bayh, and the defeated Bayh had called Lautenberg personally to rave and recommend her. Although nearly 20 others were interviewed for the job, Baum got it.

With Checchi and Lubalin holding forth over legislative matters, Lautenberg's AA and former campaign manager, Tim Ridley, 28, was exerting an enormous amount of influence over the new staff. Lautenberg made it clear that he likes to be free to deal with legislation, press matters, and affairs of state. That left Ridley with the determination of staff salaries, raises, positions, titles, and squabbles. Lautenberg never knew exactly how much money most of his staffers made, when they had a beef about their salaries, they were supposed to go to Ridley, not the senator. One staffer, feeling that Ridley wasn't responding adequately to a grievance, once said he'd go to the senator with it. Ridley told him that that was his prerogative, but that he should know Lautenberg would probably find it vulgar and wouldn't be likely to undermine his own trust in Ridley over a measly $2,000. It would also prove to Lautenberg, always the management expert, that the staffer was misreading the senator's administrative style, and confusing the kind of things that he as a member wanted to be involved with and the kinds of things he wanted to delegate to his AA.

Relationships between senators from the same state, even if they belong to the same party, meanwhile, can be notoriously strained and combative; both want their constituents to look to them when they need something from Washington, and although they never really have to vie for the same vote in the same year, members still think of themselves as competing for popularity. For Lautenberg and his counterpart, Bill Bradley, the relationship had been slightly rocky, due in large part to the fact that Bradley had been virtually the only senator representing the state over the past four years. This came about because of the indictment and censure of Harrison Williams and the decision of Williams' replacement, Nicholas Brady, not to run again. Bradley not only got used to being the state's only senator, he liked it.

Additionally, Bradley never expected to be serving with Lautenberg. Lautenberg's victory over the colorful and beloved Millicent Fenwick was the biggest upset in the 1982 Senate elections, and it meant that Bradley would be working with an ambitious, aggressive novice at the start of a political career. Even though he was enjoying the fruits of a national reputation, one that Lautenberg might never have, and even though he was considerably younger than his new colleague, ambition and eagerness make for skepticism and weariness. Lautenberg considered Checchi and her expertise important allies in the fight for attention that would be waged against Bradley.

Bradley was hardly soft competition. That many still pictured him in his basketball jersey—thus, a jock—was one of the prevailing ironies of the Senate. A devoutly serious legislator, maybe even too serious, Bradley is a student who devours facts and doesn't like to be caught short. Every night he takes a duffel bag of papers home, and his favorite legislative project, the Herculean one of revising the tax code, is indicative of his enthusiasm for detailed analysis.

Lautenberg's staff is young and eager; Bradley's is more seasoned. Bradley likes to be surrounded by older aides (over 35, that is) and the average age of his senior staff is 40 plus. Yet Bradley still writes his own speeches and saves the final word on issues for himself. Bradley's workload is also higher because New Jerseyans are still in the habit of turning to him—he is receiving more than 10,000 letters a week compared to Lautenberg's 5,000. It came as no surprise to anyone who knew him to learn that Lautenberg wanted that to change. Lautenberg had been the absolute center of his corporate world; he was not about to start learning the second fiddle's part now.

Meanwhile, though, Lautenberg still has homework to do, and Checchi is the perfect tutor. The subject has been the budget process, and Checchi, who has a methodical, deliberate way of explaining things, is ready with charts and graphs with which to instruct the eager tyro. There will be several of these sessions. After all, as Checchi says, the budget process is "a very arcane thing."

Checchi has drawn several flow charts to aid in her explanations. The problem for the teacher is that Lautenberg has what she calls "a businessman's mind"; while his business background is helpful in some ways, Lautenberg tends to see the word "budget" and think in rational terms. He views the charts as representing input and output processes. "But this is a whole different bag," Checchi explains. Lautenberg is looking at it too rationally. He has to look at it more existentially. Or something.

No matter how much time Checchi has with her pupil today, she knows she will need more. Neither the lengthy menu nor the graphs could make immediate sense for the newcomer. Checchi knows the simple truth Lautenberg will eventually learn: that the budget process is a bitch. Few on Capitol Hill understand it, fewer still want to deal with it; yet almost everyone in Congress has to take a whack at it sooner or later. The budget process is like a disease for which Congress keeps trying to find a cure, and which the White House keeps trying to bring under control. For as long as there is a Congress, there will be complaints about the budget.

Checchi has her work cut out for her.

At 12:45, as James McClure calls the Senate Republican conference he chairs to order for a special caucus in the Dirksen hearing room on the budget resolution, it dawns on Howard Baker that the cards aren't being dealt the way he would like. Compromise is not in the air. Unity is not in the air. Typically, Baker has been hoping all along that some eleventh-hour unifying force would materialize to bring agreement about. Now it is the eleventh hour, and the force is not with Howard Baker. He can see it all in the faces of those sitting around the table. Almost all the members present, even newly arrived freshmen, have budget resolutions of their own, each containing some salient element they are refusing to deal on. The battleground is divided into three major ideological camps: those who would rather die than tax; those who believe that the budget should be balanced by cutting domestic spending; and those who think Cap Weinberger has gone hog wild with his defense requests.

Nearly all the Republican members are on hand, but only a few staffers—including, of course, Range and Bell. McClure introduces Baker, who begins by saying that the session is "an extraordinary opportunity to exchange ideas," even though he privately feels that he has already heard enough ideas to last a lifetime. Baker is interrupted by a request from the back of the room that the conference be held behind closed doors. McClure nods, and the doors are shut. Baker tells the group that even though the budget resolution could be brought up for consideration on the Senate floor under the rules the next day, he won't call it up until Monday, so as to give everybody a chance to voice opinions and get the Republican act together. "Pete is the expert in these matters," Baker says, turning the floor over to Domenici. Baker will not talk again in the hour-long meeting, even though more than a dozen senators do voice concerns—a sign that he has reached the point of exasperation.

Baker has little ammunition at his disposal with which to facilitate an agreement; he knows it, they know it. He has never been one to threaten—a fact that is sometimes misread as passivity or weakness—but even if he felt in the mood for a threat, it is clear that not much would come of it. Senators feel more obligated to be individualistic in cases like this than they do to be part of a team. The exercise in party loyalty that many went through in 1981 with kicks and screams was exhausting and ego-straining, and Baker has had to realize many times since that he cannot force members into going along with something they have already made up their minds against. Baker and Domenici know that no party agreement will be produced in the caucus. Baker hopes those who want

116

to get out front and take a stance will do so this week; then he will be able to make a stronger pitch to get them on board next week when the resolution actually comes before the Senate.

Bell meanwhile focuses on his boss's views. What does Domenici want to do? Or, more realistically, what does Bell want Domenici to do? Both men feel a need to prove to their Republican colleagues that they did not sell out to the Democrats in committee when they passed the resolution the White House and the leadership hated; they want to show that they were defending a budget process that was in grave danger. Range, meanwhile, just listens. He is sizing up the various forces he will be dealing with next week on the floor, and although Baker can read political minds better than anybody in the room, Range's insights do help.

An hour later Baker, showing no outward signs of vexation, is back on the Senate floor, ready to pick up the microphone at his desk to bring the Senate back into session after the recess for the caucus. Before him are three pages written by a staff member, in response to an observation Baker had made earlier that it is a beautiful day outside. Baker didn't just say it was a beautiful day; he said he wanted to say something on the floor about it being a beautiful day. As majority leader, he performs some procedural functions not unlike those of the host of a TV talk show. Some days he opens with the Senate equivalent of a Johnny Carson monologue. It's part of his mandated effort to keep spirits as high as possible, his own included. Now he reads the statement prepared for him, pausing every once in a while to ad lib an observation of his own. "I just walked from the Dirksen office building across the east ellipse of the Capitol grounds to the Senate steps," he says, departing from the text. "I would estimate the temperature is about 85 degrees, the grass is freshly mowed, the air is soft and sweet, the sunshine is penetrating, and it confirms what I have always believed, and that is, winter should be a place that you visit and not a season of the year.

"I am tempted, Mr. President, to ask that the Senate adjourn itself to the front lawn of the Capitol and conduct our business there. But on further thought it struck me that if I get 100 senators out there under those salubrious circumstances, it would be impossible to keep a quorum." Baker seems to be getting more pleasure out of discussing nature than out of negotiating budgets; who could blame him?

Later, the temperature climbs to a freakishly warm 88 degrees, and Baker, who is chatting in his private office with Stuart Spencer, a principal architect of the Reagan victory in 1980, takes a moment to gaze out the window at the blossoming trees of spring. The moment is interrupted by word from the Senate floor. The troops are restless for news on the schedule, and Greene reports that an agreement on the bankruptcy bill is within reach.

Baker excuses himself and makes the one-minute walk into the Senate chamber, a walk he has made too many times to count. As leader, he often must dash onto the floor like a paramedic rushing to some stricken victim. The nature of floor activity begs disaster. With the majority of senators largely ignorant of Senate procedure, and with old and more traditional debating styles evaporating, snags routinely develop. Sometimes a member surprises the leadership with a previously unannounced delaying ploy; more often, however, difficulties arise because staff is working with staff and acting on behalf of members who will not always subsequently agree to the arrangements made in their behalf. It's enough to give Baker fits.

But this afternoon Baker has some good news for a change. "Mr. President," he all but shouts in excitement, "all things come to those who wait. We have waited a long time, and I have long since agreed to settle for far less than all things. But we have an agreement, I believe."

Yes, after nearly two years of tangles and hassles, Baker moves to debate on two bankruptcy reform bills, one that would restore a federal bankruptcy court system declared unconstitutional and one that would make it harder for consumers to cancel their debts. Thurmond, and the judiciary committee he chairs, have been attempting to pass the bankruptcy bill since it was first reported from the committee in September of 1981, with no success. The reform package has encountered a series of delays, especially those resulting from disagreements over the consumer provisions and appointment provisions for bankruptcy judges that are part of the bill. But behind-the-scenes maneuvering by the staffs of Howard Metzenbaum, Democrat of Ohio, and Robert Dole, who chairs the courts subcommittee, are finally paying off, permitting both sides to save face and the bill to come before the full Senate at last.

In this way, the bankruptcy bill is a typical piece of legislation. Most of the difficult issues have been worked out ahead of time, because there is not enough time in the Senate schedule for exhaustive debate and compromise by the Senate as a whole. One of the first questions Baker will ask a chairman after a request is made for a reported bill to come to the Senate floor is, "How much time will it take?"

Major reform in the bankruptcy field hasn't been addressed by the full Senate in over five years. Today it will take up 3 hours and 15 minutes of the Senate's time, and will pass on a voice vote. Most of the members do not speak on the bill; of those who do, most simply ask that their statements be placed in the record as if read. During what is supposed to be debate on the bankruptcy bill, there will be more members of the judiciary committee staff on the floor than there will be senators.

At 5:50, one long buzzer sounds throughout Senate domain, so loudly it can be heard in the bathrooms of the Senate office buildings. It announces that a roll call vote is beginning, and now, for the first time, the galleries will be able to see the Senate in action. There are 15 minutes allowed for a roll call vote, but that doesn't mean exactly 15 minutes. It is up to Greene and his Democratic counterpart Patrick Griffin, the secretary for the minority, to have the cloakrooms notify all members that a vote is coming up; senators are so worried about their voting records that missing one is considered a great calamity. Sometimes votes will be postponed while a member comes in from an airport or from a lunch downtown; at other times the votes, if they are set to begin at a given hour, will start on time but will be delayed until an absent member shows up. The cloakroom has all the pressure of trying to get everyone there on time. Seven and a half minutes after the first bell, the clerk reads the roll, separating the yeas and the nays. Then five bells go off, signifying that there are only 7½ minutes left. Under normal procedure, the five bells go off again and a rush of members come through the doors from the elevators, many of them in groups because they get off the subway cars in the basement together. Today, however, Washington weather is so uncharacteristically civil that many members eschew the subway and venture outdoors, strolling over to the Capitol on foot. Some have their coats over their shoulders for the nice, breezy JFK look politicians still love to affect.

If one trains an eye up at the gallery during a typical vote, one sees that people there are interested in what is going on. But when their heads move together, and they start to point to the floor, it's obvious that Edward Kennedy has arrived on the floor. He is still the most noticeable senator, the one whom everyone recognizes and the one who makes people feel they are really in the Capitol.

Not surprisingly, within minutes of his arrival, Kennedy is chatting with Al Simpson. Their big day is tomorrow. Even though they don't see eye to eye on the immigration matter, and most other policies, they are still in this together. In the Senate, one senator never expects he'll agree 100 percent with another senator on anything.

Both Simpson and Kennedy have come to realize that, while immigration may not be the sexiest issue ever, those who are involved and interested in the legislation, such as farmers and the Hispanic community, have definite and volatile views and feel a crucial stake in the outcome of the process.

At 6:30 P.M. Baker looks at the little index card that he carries in his inside suit pocket, and realizes he is due at a fundraising reception for Governor John Sununu of New Hampshire, hosted by Paul Laxalt and House minority leader Robert Michel. Regardless of whether Baker actually enjoys such events, he is a good soldier about attending. For fundraisers, Baker's name is just as important as his appearance. If he gives consent, organizers can list him as one of the stars who will be present, thus enticing more people to the event. This one would set guests back $250 a ticket.

The truth is that tonight will be neither Reagan's night, though he is making his big speech to the joint session—nor Dodd's, though he is answering it—but, rather, television's. The night was made for television; none of this would probably be happening if television did not exist. Reagan will be using the Congress more as a prop than as an audience; he will be speaking to the folks at home. Congress has to sit up and pay attention, though, because even though Central America never seems uppermost in the minds of the people, when TV viewers see that their president is devoting 25 minutes to it on all three networks in prime time, they will have little choice but to be interested for the duration. And with the public's interest piqued, Congress has little choice but to appear interested as well.

In the last ten years, especially, television has become an object of great dread and great allure for Congress. Some members are repelled by it, but many, many more are seduced. They come running when the little red light goes on. It offers an opportunity to prove themselves to the folks back home— thus alleviating their insecurities about losing their jobs in the next election—and can be a vehicle to national political stardom, if they know how to use it. More and more members are trying to master TV. They hire television consultants, practice the art of producing nice crisp (and brief) "sound bites" for the network news, and pay scrupulous attention to their appearance.

Most of the old-timers who scoffed at television, tried to fight it or ignore it, are gone now. The new Senate is a centipede that dances to a television tune.

Since 1978, proceedings of the House of Representatives have been televised. The president is on television almost every day, one way or another. And so, in terms of television footage, the Senate has often been the least visible corner of the triangle of House, Senate, and president. During a nationwide railroad strike in 1982, the House could be seen on television debating the issues involved and coming to an agreement to end the strike. The president was seen on TV making a speech about it. But in the eyes of the television viewer, nothing was coming out of the Senate on this crucial national matter—even though it was actually the Senate that wrote some of the original language of the agreement.

Senators are forever coming back from trips home complaining that their constituents griped about not seeing them participate in the big debate on the such-and-such bill. They didn't see their senator because they were watching the House.

The argument over whether proceedings of the Senate should be televised has been going on since the Kefauver hearings of the fifties. Baker made televising Senate floor proceedings one of his main objectives when he became majority leader. But it was the objective that got away. Why should senators, who love nothing in this world more than getting their faces in front of a TV camera and onto the screens of their home states and of the entire nation, shrink from the idea of bringing lights and cameras into the chamber? Many reasons have been put forward by the nothing-if-not-stalwart opposition to Baker's crusade.

For the most part, senators against TV say they are afraid there will be rampant grandstanding once television is admitted and that the decorum of the Senate will suffer. Senators, it is said, will get even more long-winded with their speeches than they already are. Some will try to use television in the chamber to establish national reputations and power bases. They will strut, fret, and pirouette before the camera—or so the skeptics insist.

Baker, the leader of the movement to bring cameras in,

likes to lecture his colleagues that to televise the Senate is merely to provide "a technological extension of the galleries"—to allow much of the nation the same view as the few dozen spectators who happen to be in Washington. Baker is considered a master of persuasion in the Senate. He can change minds on foreign policy or budget matters, even win support for the president when there is extreme resistance to follow along. But, for all that, he has been unable to win members over to his plans for television. Three years after he introduced the resolution to allow television in the Senate, he still does not have enough votes to win on it or to stop a sure filibuster attempt by Russell Long, Democrat of Louisiana. It illustrates not any weakness of Baker's but rather how deeply some senators fear and loathe television and its power, real or imagined.

Thus the images of the Senate most viewers continue to get are limited largely to hasty watercolors made by staff artists for the networks, interviews conducted on the Capitol grounds, and the prepared statements read into the lens from that Senate TV room with the backdrop of *Congressional Records*. Meanwhile, the trend in the last three years on the network newscasts has been to phase out news from Washington, especially that made on Capitol Hill as opposed to the White House. No longer do cameras show up at every hearing for the old three-minute spot, nor is it any longer considered nationally newsworthy every time Congress sneezes or scratches its nose, as was for years the custom when the evening newscasts went ritually to their Capitol Hill reporters whether there was news from Congress or not.

The result is paradoxical. While some members of the Senate—those who've taken their TV lessons and passed with flying colors—attract cameras and seem individually impressive on television, the Senate as a whole now labors under the reputation of being a laggardly, unproductive body. There were plenty of Congress-haters before this situation; the television imbalance may have exacerbated the problem. Senators concerned only about their own images probably aren't bothered by this; those who worry about the image of the Senate and the Congress as a whole find it frustrating, even maddening.

As the clock strikes 7:00, Howard Greene waits outside his post in the Republican cloakroom for copies of the president's speech, which are supposed to be delivered from the White House directly to him, before anyone else, so that he can give them to Republican senators. But the same thing happens all the time: while Greene waits for his copies, a reporter will sashay down the steps with one in hand. At least one network correspondent likes to call out at such times, so that Greene can plainly hear, "God, can you believe this last page?" Greene blanches. "Oh—you didn't get the speech yet?" the reporter will say. It irritates Greene tremendously and the reporters know it. This evening, word comes down from the press gallery on the third floor that some members of the press and some members of Senate staffs do indeed already have their copies, while Greene still waits for the White House courier to deliver 54 to him. Every time the phone rings, it is another Republican senator growling, "Where's my copy of the speech?" They want them early so they can prepare their reaction comments for the post-speech interviews to be carried on radio or TV stations back home.

Around the House chamber, security forces are making another in a series of electronic "sweeps" of the House floor. Strategy sessions have been going on for the past two weeks between the House sergeant at arms office, the White House advance team, the FBI, and the Secret Service, who share responsibility for the president's safety while he is on the Hill. When the president visits the Capitol, all or most of the 1,300-member Capitol Hill police force is on duty. The Capitol becomes a veritable armed camp for the evening.

At 7:30, a large CBS News trailer with a big gray eye on the side can be heard humming in the Capitol parking lot. It arrived the day before to set up shop for coverage of the president's speech. The three networks take turns handling the "pool" coverage of such events, and this speech goes to CBS.

Even though the event can be planned for in advance, the logistics of it make the preparations almost as hectic as if this were an unexpected late-breaking story. Five cameras have been set up in the House chamber, and another has been stationed across the street, on the roof of the library of Congress, to give the networks their "beauty shot" that sets the scene.

Inside the chamber, cables run along the floor, defying most of the attempts to conceal them with tape or by tucking them under the rug. During planning sessions, the House sergeant at arms negotiated the camera position for the main camera that will be trained on the president; it usually sits in the center aisle, and members have complained in the past of not being able to see around it. CBS has promised no one's view will be obstructed.

When the text of the president's speech is delivered to the CBS crew inside the trailer, an anxious havoc reigns. When it is noted that the speech contains numerous references to Nicaragua—Reagan's favorite bête noire of the moment, though not quite of evil-empire status—producers begin to plan for shots of the Nicaraguan ambassador as he sits in the diplomatic corps sections watching and presumably listening. Then word comes that the Nicaraguan chargé d'affaires, not the ambassador, will be present, and the people in the trailer realize that no one knows what he looks like. Immediately, a messenger is dispatched to the Nicaraguan embassy to retrieve a photograph of said chargé d'affaires. The license number of his car is also obtained, so it can be spotted when he arrives and his path can be traced by the CBS crew as he makes his way to his seat.

With a roar of motorcycles and city-police-car sirens accompanying him, the president arrives at the House entrance to the Capitol in his bullet-proof limousine. It is 7:37 P.M. As with most presidential motorcades, this one is 12 cars long; some are marked, others are not. In addition to the limo carrying the president, there is a decoy limo, three sedans containing about four Secret Service agents apiece, a station wagon with three security guards inside, and two more sedans carrying White House aides, the president's physician, and the military attaché who holds the "football," a briefcase containing the codes for launching a nuclear attack.

As members of the Senate and House march into the chamber, they unknowingly pass through three or four unobtrusive security checkpoints, at which security personnel who know the faces of all 535 of them make sure no imposter or intruder has joined the processional. Meanwhile, CBS producers outside in the truck are bitching because the procession of diplomats is plodding along more slowly than expected, and the appointed hour of the president's speech is imminent. But the pace then picks up, and the diplomats are in their seats on time. Last to enter are the Senate leadership aides, who are allowed to stand along the walls of the chamber during the speech. The aides have learned that the later they arrive, the closer they get to the podium.

As Mrs. Reagan takes her first-row seat in the House gallery at five minutes before eight, Janet Westmoreland, associate producer of "The CBS Evening News," stands next to the president in one of two rooms secured for him in the Speaker's office. After pointing out seat locations of people to whom the president will refer or allude in his speech, so that the CBS director will be able to get shots of them at the right time, Westmoreland's major, indeed only, responsibility now is to tell the president when to enter the House chamber for his speech. She turns to him and says, "Now, Mr. President, I will cue you," Reagan, exuding an affable calm at this point, tells her, "I'm good at taking cues."

Suddenly, with the President of the United States at her side, Westmoreland realizes that—of all things—there is, at this very moment, a large knife stashed inside her purse. She had given a birthday party for a friend in the press gallery earlier in the day, and absent-mindedly tossed the knife into the purse after cutting the cake with it. Crazily, she wonders how it would look if Secret Service agents asked her to open her purse and, upon doing so, a big gleaming knife fell out. And—how would this reflect on CBS News? Fortunately, none of that happens. She is distracted by other worries, and nobody asks her to open her purse anyway.

The timing of her cue has to be perfect, because all the networks have been told that the sergeant at arms will announce the president's arrival to the House at precisely 8:00:45, giving the networks time to flash their "Special Report" graphics on the screen and for their anchormen to do brief introductions.

At precisely 8:00:45 P.M., it happens: "Mister Speaker, the President of the United States."

Only 12 times previously in the past 25 years has a president addressed a special joint session. The president is here this time not so much to sell members of Congress on the wisdom of his policies in Central America—he knows how most of them feel—as to reach out and touch the television audience, to whom Reagan has appealed time and again during his presidency. The attempt to sail over congressional heads on the Central America issue has been dubbed a high-risk maneuver by some journalists because voter sentiment has been running strongly against U.S. involvement. But the gipper loves a challenge.

In his speech, the president pushes for a bipartisan coalition on Central America, meaning one that would support him. "The national security of all Americans is at stake," he says, and the mere $600 million in aid he wants for El Salvador amounts to "less than one-tenth of what Americans will spend this year on coin-operated video games." When he observes that Congress "shares the power and responsibility for our foreign policy," he elicits a smattering of titters from the Democratic side of the aisle, not seen or heard by the TV audience. A very fleeting bipartisan coalition does present itself when Reagan declares, "Let me say to those who invoke the memory of Vietnam: there is no thought of sending American combat troops to Central America."

For that sentiment, Reagan gets a standing ovation.

Reagan tries to make the contrasts between the governments of Nicaragua and El Salvador graphically clear. He paints them in strict good guy–bad guy terms. "Violence has been Nicaragua's most important export to the world," he says, and he characterizes the Nicaraguan government as one that has "imposed a new dictatorship" on that country. He cites a long list of its offenses, including refusing to hold promised elections, seizing control of the media, moving against the private sector and labor unions, even denying Catholic bishops and priests the right to say Mass on the radio during Holy Week. "It has insulted and mocked the Pope," Reagan says of the Nicaraguan dictatorship, and he denies the charge that those who oppose the Sandinistas are just "diehard supporters of the previous Somoza regime."

The government of El Salvador, Reagan says, is on the other hand "making every effort to guarantee democracy, free labor unions, freedom of religion, and a free press" in that country. Reagan asks rhetorically if it is to be the curse of democracies to "remain passive" and "sit by" while "threats to their security and prosperity accumulate" and while "independent nations of this hemisphere are integrated into the most aggressive empire the modern world has seen." He lobs the ball into Congress's court when he says, "I do not believe there is a majority in the Congress or the country that counsels passivity, resignation, defeatism in the face of this challenge to freedom and security in our hemisphere."

While Congress will give the president an enthusiastic reception, television viewers may perceive it as wildly approving: House Republicans have forged themselves into a gallant cheerleading battalion that roars and claps with enthusiasm at appropriate moments in the speech. And there are many appropriate moments in the speech. Away from the cheers, though, and all but alone in the Capitol TV studio, Chris Dodd is still rehearsing his speech. Dodd tries to familiarize himself with the lines as they will crawl by on the TelePrompTer. He wants this to be good. He also wants it to be definitive—even though just how official, and how Democratic, the speech really is has been and will continue to be the source of acrimonious debate within the party.

Some 90 minutes before the president began speaking, the

Dodd staff had dispatched a task force to find out what was going to be in the speech. They had expected a tougher speech than the president gave, but they couldn't find out anything until they got a copy of it with one hour to go. By then it was too late to change their own speech, because of the time it takes to reprogram a TelePrompTer. They would stick with their all-purpose opening line. "Good evening," Dodd would say. "Unfortunately, tonight the president gave a speech intended to bring people to their feet, not to their senses."

Mike Naylor and Robert Dockerty, Dodd's key aides, had been displeased to discover that Reagan would be quoting Democrat Harry Truman; Dodd had taken a Dwight D. Eisenhower quote out of the final version of his speech.

Dodd had asked pollster Patrick Caddell to ascertain the public mood regarding Central America; he wanted to know if he could get away with a "hard," aggressive speech. Caddell was big on the Vietnam analogy, claiming that Americans were becoming increasingly wary of the similarities. Luckily for Dodd, the Vietnam theme would not be stressed in the final draft of his speech. Reagan would be stealing the thunder on that with his own reference to Vietnam and the accompanying pledge that no American combat troops would be sent to Central America—or at least that there was "no thought" of sending any.

Dodd, Naylor, and Mike McAdams, a personal friend of Dodd's, had gone over the speech again line by line just before dinner that night. Naylor's big worry, as the clock ticks by and the president winds down, is that the man operating the hand crank on Dodd's TelePrompTer, not having worked with Dodd before, doesn't know his pace. He may crank too slow, he may crank too fast. It could trip Dodd up. But the cranking proceeds at the right pace. At least in terms of delivery, Dodd will not be left with egg on his face.

Dodd's 20-minute speech is carried live by all three networks. His Democratic colleagues watch it on TV in the Senate cloakroom or in their offices. On the air, Dodd looks rather lonely standing behind a podium in an empty room, in contrast to the Reagan performance before a joint session, surrounded by the full panoply of presidential pomp. As for Dodd's speech, it turns out to be roughly as controversial as Rob Lebatore, the Democratic policy committee staff director, had been warned it would be five days earlier, when he first suggested Dodd's name for the job.

Where some Democrats feel Dodd goes wrong is in appearing to be too soft on Communists, too harsh on the administration. Much of the speech is given over to dramatic recitations of conditions in Central America as Dodd observed them in his travels. He speaks of most people being "appallingly poor" and of the region as being "racked with poverty," "racked with hunger," and "racked with injustices." These conditions, not the Soviets, are to blame for revolutionary foment, Dodd says. "Unless those oppressive conditions change, that region will continue to seethe with revolution—with or without the Soviets," Dodd says. To some, it sounds as if Dodd has let the Russians off scot-free.

In addition, Dodd as much as charges the U.S. government with "association with criminals" and emotionally describes the situation as he witnessed it during one of his trips to El Salvador: "I know about the morticians who travel the streets each morning to collect the bodies of those summarily dispatched the night before by Salvadoran security forces—gangland style—the victim on bended knee, thumbs wired behind the back, a bullet through the brain."

Reaction to Dodd's speech begins almost as soon as the speech does. Phones in his Senate office light up. One of the first callers says something along the lines of, "Get that commie off the air." But when the broadcast is over, Dodd himself seems pleased. He and those around him think it was a darn good speech. They close up shop and go home. Later, they will hear from those who don't think the speech was quite so darn good as they do.

Nancy Kassebaum of Kansas would say later, "I think I probably didn't disagree so much with what was said from a policy standpoint as I think it was said wrong. And then the timing was terrible—to follow the president and berate him in very strong language, and really in a rather demagogic approach, attack what the president said, and sort of hype it from the other side. That was what was done."

President Reagan doesn't get only raves on his performance, however. Not surprisingly, Joseph Biden, Democrat of Delaware, is unimpressed by the speech. "I was thinking, 'How in the hell did he get elected?' " he would recall later. "I was thinking, 'What are we doing?' I was thinking, 'There is a fundamental gap in generations here.' I mean, maybe the problem is that his view of the world is dictated by the place in which he's stood the last 30 years."

Patrick Leahy of Vermont, looking back on the speech, said, "I keep a daily journal, and I sat down and made notes about the speech. Here we had the opportunity, I felt, to really spell out a policy, because all the Central American countries were going to be listening, as well as the American people. I thought how unfortunate it was that something that was going to affect our relationship with this hemisphere for decades to come was being treated like some public relations thing."

The *Washington Post* would headline its report on that night's reactions to the president's speech with the words "Support, Skepticism." Support came from such predictable sources as John Tower of Texas, who said, "The president made a compelling case of our need to come to terms with the critical situation in Central America." But House foreign affairs committee chairmen Dante B. Fascell of Florida and Michael D. Barnes of Maryland both said, the *Post* reported, that they felt "Reagan had failed to forge bipartisan support for his Central American plan."

The presidential motorcade had long since done its usual wending down Pennsylvania Avenue to the White House. As it did, President Reagan may have looked back over his shoulder at the Capitol dome, which gleams a vibrant, almost unreal bright white under the lights thrown on it after dark. Far below the dome, though, there is an unforeseen center of Capitol activity: a crack in the government that Reagan could not have perceived. Actually, it is a crack in the façade of the Capitol building itself. At 10:30, Capitol architect George White receives a call informing him that a 16-foot section of the historic West Front has broken loose from the wall and crashed to the ground below, leaving large chunks of sandstone veneer toppled in a heap outside the last visible section of the original Capitol building.

The following morning, with the pile of rubble lying outside the building, the Senate subcommittee on legislative branch appropriations, which oversees expenditures for the Capitol building, will be meeting inside.

It will not be a joyous occasion. It will not even be friendly. The chairman of the subcommittee, Alfonse D'Amato of New York, furious that he has been moved to the new Hart Senate office building, is smarting over proposals from the architect's office to extend, not restore, the West Front.

Capitol architect White, the target of D'Amato's wrath, had been scheduled to testify before the subcommittee earlier in the week; but his appearance had to be delayed. So, thanks to a stroke of colossal bad luck, White will appear the morning after a part of the Capitol has fallen, dramatically, to the ground.

4

⌒⌒

THURSDAY

*It was my experience in the early days that you could count on
somebody's word from the beginning on a vote. They'd stick
with it, even if it was going to affect them adversely. You
didn't figure they were liars. Now, there are more members
who are less reliable. They're very honest when they give you
their word, but they don't hesitate to change it later on.*

ROBERT PACKWOOD (R-ORE.)

Chris Dodd awakens early. The fact that he is to appear
on national television again is enough to coax him out of bed
even after a thoroughly exhausting night. He is in demand
now, and if the last 24 hours have proven anything to him, it
is that he loves attention. Maybe that's why he became a senator.

Sitting on the set of NBC's "Today" show, Dodd looks
more sure of himself than he did the night before. The
pressure is less. Maybe it is because he isn't following the president's show, or maybe because there is no TelePrompTer to
worry about. When asked by correspondent Judy Woodruff
about the president's speech, Dodd replies, "I did detect a lit-

tle softening," but soon manages to squeeze in what he has really come to say: "If we think that simply spending billions and billions and billions or more into El Salvador is going to bring about the safety of the United States, that's a terribly simplistic view, and not a very accurate one." He leaves the studios confident that the interview has gone well for him.

The decision that had been made the previous Friday by a handful of Senate staffers, assigning to Dodd responsibility for making the Democratic response to a presidential address, has changed the freshman's standing in the Senate, immediately and permanently. By the time Dodd arrives at his office, earlier than usual, queries from the press are already overwhelming him. He has never received so many in one morning. Dodd's speech last night has pinpointed him as the leader of the opposition to the president's policies in Central America, so the networks consider him ripe for the interviewing; his good looks and lucidity don't hurt either. With 99 faces to compete against, it is only through extraordinary events and statements that a member can break from the pack. This week, Dodd has made his break.

In the Capitol, where rumor mills are studies in perpetual motion and loose talk wafts through corridors like Muzak, what would be mere idle gossip elsewhere takes on an added, exalted status as, potentially, tomorrow's news. On this Thursday morning in the Capitol, it is not Dodd's speech that is the principal topic of hallway prattle. Nor are people joking and murmuring about who is, or aspires to be, sleeping with whom, nor about how one staffer or another has managed to navigate another rung on the ladder of success. They are instead chortling over the fact that last night part of the Capitol building fell down in a heap.

Since the crumbling occurred at a very late hour—too late for the evening newscasts—it still has the status of in-house poop, something none but the knowing know. Small crowds of Hill regulars gather at the sight of the collapse, competing for space with media beings, coming and going in shifts and sharing not so much shock as bemusement. It seems so graphic a symbol of something, something basic about the institution and the travails that go on within it.

Range, aware that Capitol architect George White is to testify this morning before Senator Alfonse D'Amato's subcommittee, is particularly tickled. So is anyone else who remembers when D'Amato got assigned to the Hart building. D'Amato took the news like an election defeat. Terrified that his constituents would think he was living in the lap of luxury if he moved into the new clubhouse, D'Amato devised a plan whereby the sergeant at arms would send the Capitol police to his office in the Dirksen building, and, in front of a New York TV station crew, forcibly transport him, in his chair, to the new building. But rules committee chairman Charles Mathias rejected the scheme, because "I didn't think it was appropriate for a United States senator to be manhandled by the police."

By 9:30, S-126 in the Capitol is packed for the legislative branch appropriations hearing. The turnout practically constitutes a mob, at least as compared to the handful that normally materializes for such hearings. Obviously they are attracted, like Romans to the Coliseum, by the prospect of a battle: D'Amato, whose feelings about the architect are well known, versus White, who arrives with seven cronies in tow.

Also on hand is assistant majority leader Ted Stevens, who had specifically asked that the White appearance be delayed until today so he can be present. He wanted the opportunity to attack White over a new 40,000-pound sculpture planned for the Madison building of the Library of Congress. Stevens can't quite see the wisdom of blacking out 20 percent of the total window area of the entire library annex for a damn sculpture. Architecture critic Wolf Von Eckhardt has agreed, suggesting in the *Washington Post* that hanging the sculpture might constitute a "book-hater's revenge for the cost of the Library—dimming the only sizable source of natural light in this entire 1.4 million-square-foot box." D'Amato reads that remark into the record during the hearing.

However loathed, the sculpture is not to be the focus of the debate. That will be left to D'Amato's antipathy toward White over the notoriously extravagant Hart building, which he has been forced to move into, and the continuing controversy concerning the future of the Capitol's West Front. As with most but not all problems on the Hill, the latter has two distinctly opposite solutions: expansion or restoration. Each option has what amounts to an armed camp rallying for its cause.

Speaker O'Neill and White advocate expanding or extending the West Front by 147,000 gross square feet at a cost estimated in 1983 to be $73 million (and certain to be much more by the time the project, if approved, is finished). O'Neill and White are not thinking entirely and unselfishly of history. They are thinking of the future, and of creature comforts, themselves being the creatures to comfort. Their plans for the new quarters call for hideaway offices for senators and representatives, new committee rooms, and new members-only restaurant space. O'Neill once defended the expansion plan by saying, "We don't have very good facilities for dining here. You could put a real first-class dining room in." Tip knows the way to a taxpayer's heart.

Those, like Baker, who support restoration—and they include the National Trust for Historic Preservation and the American Institute of Architects—argue that the "historic continuity" of the Capitol would be defaced by the expansionists and their first-class dining room and that there is no "urgent" need for the added office and committee-room space.

Most new arrivals come to Congress to talk about water projects back home or to wrestle with the Russians. But they quickly learn that the affairs of the architect's office, and so many other affairs of offices they have never heard of, often intrude on schedules and staff time, and that part of the job is to see that attention is paid. Attention must be paid.

The problem of the West Front goes way, way back—about 185 years, as long as it has existed. Burned by the British in 1814, caught in the middle of another fire in 1851, the West Front then subsequently suffered less traumatic but no-less-ravaging effects of deterioration. Even before the collapse the previous night, specialists had proclaimed the West Front structurally unsound. Now, it is just another sticky problem that appears on Baker's clock as majority leader.

Many of those at today's hearing think the advance publicity, suggesting a D'Amato–White grudge match, has been exaggerated. After all, as chairman of the subcommittee, D'Amato is responsible for looking at and presenting arguments in favor of and in opposition to funding measures, then taking the data from the hearings and making his decisions and recommendations. They don't see his role as that of a Capitol Hill gunslinger with White at the top of the hit list.

But that may be how D'Amato sees it, at least on the issue of the West Front and its fate. This is to be a classic display of an increasingly common Senate syndrome: a member approaching a question with his mind already made up. Nobody really stands a chance this morning of nudging D'Amato away from the view he has held since before he walked into the committee room—certainly not White, who has even gone to the essentially futile trouble of bringing a little plastic model of the proposed new front along with him to the hearing.

D'Amato had sold himself to voters on the basis of his leadership abilities and fiscal conservatism, not his expertise at office relocation and housekeeping. But the realities of the modern Senate are such that he and other members end up spending an inordinate, even incredible, amount of time on this kind of "urgent" national problem. When such people dream of becoming senators, they do not picture things like this.

Range is frustrated that he doesn't have the time to get over to watch the spectacle. But he will get great pleasure from learning what happened and reporting it to Baker. Range will be getting the unexpurgated version from colleagues—not the censored version that will appear when the proceedings of the subcommittee's hearings are published.

Official transcripts could not and would not do justice to D'Amato's harangue. After the hearing, it would be the sub-committee staff director Don Massey's duty to clean up D'Amato's remarks for the record. This great senatorial privilege permits anything that is said to be erased from the permanent account. Then, unless it has been captured on film or tape, it will exist only in the memory of those who heard it. In a way, it is truth that becomes gossip, as opposed to the other way around.

At the moment that D'Amato is demolishing the Hart building, brick by brick (although, of course, it isn't made of anything so prosaic as bricks), Mary Jane Checchi is attending to Lautenberg, who is sitting at yet another session of the banking committee—this one to consider the topics of IMF quota increases and the Export-Import Bank legislation, the kinds of issues that may seem deathly dull to outsiders but inside are hotly politicized and engender wrangling and maneuvering. The banking committee will have to share control over the complicated matters with the foreign relations committee and a host of other members once the bill gets to the Senate floor.

For Checchi, tutoring the new senator, this isn't a nice, clean way to start off. The bills are complex; they have been reported to both the banking committee and the foreign relations committee. Checchi is aware that the two bills also have notorious legislative histories, and that Lautenberg should be prepared for messy complications. The two have gone over the material several times, Lautenberg proving himself an industrious pupil, but Checchi wishes he could have cut his teeth on something more basic, less byzantine. Lautenberg has made it clear to her that he doesn't want to be left in the dark about anything, yet she is having a tough time helping him stake out a position of influence on an issue so heavily trod by others. Senators with seniority may long since have adopted such issues as their own, and be reluctant to surrender any turf. Garn, Proxmire, and others on the committee have been working for years on the IMF measures; a freshman senator can't just walk in and order the veterans aside every two years when the authorization reappears. Checchi counsels her boss to be patient. He is good enough. His time will come.

Lautenberg, too, would probably rather have been throwing his two cents into the D'Amato brawl over at the Capitol building. He hasn't been terribly happy with his accommodations on the Hill, either. Since his election, Lautenberg and his staff have been operating from temporary quarters in the Russell office building, while waiting for a suite in the Hart building to be completed. Checchi and the rest of the legislative team are crowded together in one room. For the last two months, Lautenberg has been haggling with the architect's office over the space he is scheduled to get. The size of a senator's staff is supposed to correspond to the size of the member's state population, and the size of staff determines how much office space he will get. But Bradley was awarded his space previously, and Lautenberg was very displeased to learn that his New Jersey colleague had more than Lautenberg would be getting. This poses logistical problems for his operation, yes, but maybe worse, it is a blow to his ego. In matters of ego, senators are not markedly different from divas or movie stars. It's the nature of the Hill.

Lautenberg likes the Hart building; he considers it modern, functional, orderly. What he doesn't like is the prospect of getting bogged down in territorial squabbles. Like a graduate of est (which he is not), he wants his own space. Lautenberg feels that this issue is so commanding in its importance that he has gone to Checchi's old boss, minority leader Robert Byrd, to discuss it with him; he has even called rules committee chairman Charles Mathias, who oversees the allocations. This, of course, is upstart comportment—a freshman petitioning senior members with such matters. It's the kind of thing that would not have happened 15 years ago in the Senate. The code of behavior was stricter then. But the real problem is that there is no one to guide Lautenberg along this particular bureaucratic path. He has been acting on instinct—

the instincts of a businessman accustomed to getting his way. In the past week, though, Lautenberg has eased off complaining about the situation; he figures out that there will be innumerable matters in the months and years ahead that will get his dander up, and he doesn't want to squander his energies on something like this—or risk alienating his new colleagues so soon.

At about the time circus maximus is getting under way in D'Amato's hearing room, Howard Baker arrives in his office fresh from another $2,000 speaking engagement, this time to the executive officers and board of directors of the Whirlpool Corporation at the Watergate Hotel. Baker sits down at the conference table instead of going directly into his private office next door—his signal to all present that the morning staff meeting is about to start.

Range, as his first order of morning business, warns Baker that the D'Amato hearing may get a little rowdy. "You got some roosters in the henhouse this morning, boss," he says, in purest Rangese. But Baker is not intimidated. It's pretty hard to intimidate him, particularly since he has been chasing roosters from henhouses for years. He knows there is little he can do to change the course of this hearing anyway. As with so many crises he has had to deal with in the Senate, he will focus his energies on damage control rather than prevention. Attempting prevention in this case would be pointless.

It is 9:40; the Senate will be called into session in 20 minutes. Range knows that Baker will have to be on hand, as always, and he is anxious to get his marching orders for the day. He moves his legs back and forth under the conference table restlessly, and takes deep puffs on his cigarette.

Baker has two things on his mind this morning. First, the ongoing struggle with the budget resolution. At this point, each day seems to bring only more bad news, usually in the form of yet another compromise plan by a Republican, which really translates into another position that has to be taken into account in the course of solidifying ranks. A working group that was set up by yesterday's caucus will report back to Baker on its progress, if any. Domenici and Baker talked late last night from their homes, both of them hanging up with the impression that something dramatic would have to happen, and soon, if they were ever to revise the resolution to the point that their president and reputations are satisfied.

The second item on Baker's internal agenda is Simpson's immigration bill. Alan Cranston of California is still threatening to filibuster the motion to proceed; Baker finds this exasperating. Baker likes the floor schedule to be as productive as possible; he knows the immigration issue is a quagmire and that he won't be able to pass a bill today, but he also remembers that Simpson has told him that he is ready to go, and that the issue is receiving a great deal of attention in the media. This is as good a time as any to start debating the whole mess. William Hildenbrand, the Senate secretary, and Howard Greene, secretary for the majority, both say that Baker shouldn't allow others to push him off the track; Baker agrees. He looks around the room, thinks about Cranston, and says, "Well, we're gonna take it up anyway, and we'll stay late if we have to." He adds, "Maybe even tomorrow."

The prospect of staying late tonight doesn't noticeably ruffle very many feathers. Since becoming majority leader, Baker has made Thursday night the "late night." But the prospect of being in session on a Friday really hit a nerve, particularly with the likes of Greene and Hildenbrand, who rarely stop by on days the Senate is not in session. When reminded that he, along with most of the Republican side of the aisle, is due at a fundraiser for Senator Tower in Texas tomorrow, Baker just smiles, and says, "Keep that one quiet."

Tommy Griscom, the press secretary, stands up, a signal that it is time to march to the floor and open the Senate. As Baker enters the chamber, reporters who are chatting with Byrd once again shuffle over to Baker's desk to get a prime spot. "Will the president's speech save the aid package?" "Are you and Senator Domenici going to the White House today?" "What time will the immigration bill be taken up?"

Baker lets the questions come all at once. He knows what to say, but sees there isn't time to answer properly. A loud bell rings through the chamber, and the reporters are hustled out.

Following another prayer from the chaplain, Baker lays out the order of procedure, and his desire to bring up the immigration bill. "I had been advised that there may be an objection to proceeding to that," Baker says. "It is the intention of the leadership, notwithstanding, to stay later, and we will debate the motion to proceed tomorrow; we will debate the motion to proceed on Saturday if necessary."

If the possibility of a long bad Friday had caused alarm, the prospect of shlepping to the Senate on Saturday has, paradoxically, caused amusement. No one listening to Baker really believes he will bring the Senate in on a Saturday just to begin argument on the immigration bill. He saves those weekend get-togethers for the biggies, like increasing the debt ceiling or passing another continuing resolution to keep the government running. Anyway, secretary for the minority Pat Griffin laughs his way up to Range, and lets it be known that he too knows about the Tower fundraiser in Texas tomorrow; there is just no way Baker is going to jeopardize that. What Baker is really trying to do is simply let everyone know that this is important to him. A little idle threatening doesn't hurt.

Baker then commends the president for his speech of the previous night, as is good manners for the majority leader to do, and asks unanimous consent that the text of the speech be printed in the *Congressional Record*, not exactly a controversial proposal. That is followed by Byrd's commendation of Dodd, and his request that the Dodd speech be placed in the record as well.

Baker and Byrd chat together for a moment. Then Baker leaves to do what is for him an extraordinary thing—attend a meeting of a committee of which he is a member. Since becoming majority leader, Baker has only attended meetings of the environment and public works and foreign relations committees when his vote is absolutely necessary. Cran Montgomery, who is his legislative assistant on the foreign relations committee, thinks it is absolutely necessary today; he told Triplett to put the meeting on Baker's schedule.

Baker enters the hearing room and sits at chairman Charles Percy's immediate right, as befits his seniority. Since he has been in this seat so seldom since becoming majority leader, he is practically afforded guest-star status on this occasion. Other senators and staff members come up to greet him as if he'd just returned from abroad. All through the week, committee staffers have been nagging other committee members to attend today's session so that work on the FY84 foreign aid bill can begin. Attendance is good—Baker's presence helped with that.

Foreign aid, in the form of economic and military assistance, is a perennially prickly issue for members. They certainly want to be perceived as voting in support of American allies, and they like to give the impression that they think in global terms, but they are also aware that, particularly in times of budget reductions, a dollar spent abroad is one that can't be spent at home. Happily for members, such matters can't be decided without foreign travel to the countries seeking aid. Co-Dels (short for Congressional Delegations) are extremely popular escape mechanisms for members and staff, who are delighted to find themselves welcomed like heroes and treated like potentates in countries courting American assistance.

Since Percy took over as chairman in 1981, the foreign relations committee has failed to win approval of a single foreign aid bill. In FY82 and FY83, supplemental foreign aid was granted without authorization, by continuing resolution. Today, the committee will try to improve its luck and its reputation by voting on economic and military assistance for Israel and Egypt.

Once, this whole process was simpler. The foreign relations committee really was the presiding force behind foreign policy decisions in the Senate. But now the committee's name has become one that nobody drops. Baker knows that this perceived transformation of the foreign relations committee into impotency means there is a vacuum at the heart of the Senate—one that, sooner or later, nearly every senator will take a whack at filling. Freshmen, both on and off the committee, have been sponsoring foreign policy bills that 15 years ago would have been considered well beyond their reach and grasp. When Senate leaders attempt to coordinate foreign policy initiatives and resolutions with the White House, they are now unable, as once they commonly were able, to sit down with the leaders of the foreign relations committee—or even with the full membership of the committee. Now they must consult practically everyone in the Senate.

While the foreign relations committee may have been considered one of the most diminished fraternities on the Hill, it was hardly without its attractions and rewards to those staff members who did pledge it. One who has mastered the system and taken full advantage of it is legislative assistant Montgomery, son of a well-connected Tennessee businessman (and thus well connected himself), and a man who doesn't fit the traditional model of Baker staffers. Most of them have learned that the way to Baker's heart is to implement and expand upon Baker's own ideas. Montgomery does just the opposite. An incurable foreign policy devotee, he hatches his own ideas and tries to force them on Baker. A lot of senators would probably love this kind of gonzo attitude, but it doesn't quite work with Baker. Many of Baker's staff have watched as the senator winced under the weight of Montgomery's voluminous memos, or heard him ask Triplett, upon looking at his schedule and seeing that Montgomery has set up yet another meeting with Ambassador Somebody of Somewhere, "Do I have to?"

Indeed, Baker once told Cannon to fire Montgomery, and Cannon carried out the boss's wish. But Baker hates firing people; almost immediately, he relented. Cannon was put in the rather humiliating position of having to break the bad news and then the good news to Montgomery within the same week. Many people would have retreated into the woodwork, at least momentarily, after something like that, but to his credit, Montgomery went blissfully on. He began compiling itineraries for himself, rising to the challenge of setting new records in hopscotching the globe, exercising one of the most dearly cherished privileges of Senate staff by taking one taxpayer-financed trip after another.

In 1982, for example, Montgomery logged tens of thousands of air miles. In January of that year he visited Panama, Argentina, Chile, Peru, and Mexico. In April he dropped in on Saudi Arabia, Lebanon, Jordan, and Israel. In May he limited himself to China and Hong Kong. In October he buzzed through Kuwait, Lebanon, Tunisia, Jordan, Israel, Syria, and Iraq. Many wonder what he does as an official representative of the U.S. Senate, and it's not quite clear. During one of his trips to Lebanon, however, Montgomery paid an official, Baker-sanctioned visit to Yasir Arafat, even though the United States does not recognize the PLO.

All this travel followed 1981 trips to Kuwait, Iraq, Jordan, Spain, Saudi Arabia, Egypt, and Portugal, and two trips to Israel. Montgomery's dog-eared passport attests to the fact that there are highly coveted and little known fringe benefits that go with serving on Senate staffs, and that staff members play a greater role in domestic and even international affairs than may be realized by the press and the public. What Montgomery does is by no means considered improper conduct on the Hill. He would have been more ostracized if he had failed to take advantage of the available free travel, which enhanced his expertise and reputation.

While the foreign relations committee prepares to vote on the foreign aid package for Israel—Baker votes with the majority to increase military and economic aid to the ally beyond the levels recommended by the White House—Alan Simpson is winding up a meeting with some of his Wyoming constituents. He is predictably edgy about the immigration bill's debut this afternoon, and is anxious to run through all the final preparations that his staff has planned for him. It is a tremendously complicated issue, with a tortured past.

Prior to 1928, the rule in the United States concerning immigration was essentially that anybody who got here, stayed here. In his book *A Nation of Immigrants*, President Kennedy quoted George Washington on immigration policy: "The bosom of America is open to receive not only the opulent and respectable stranger, but the oppressed and persecuted of all nations and religions." In the first two decades of this century, Washington and Kennedy's concept of a proper immigration policy was reflected in the panorama of faces that regularly flooded Ellis Island. But in the 1920s the bosom began to close. And the golden door as well: entry into America became regulated according to a national-origin quota system, which allowed entree of immigrant groups in proportion to the current composition of the U.S. population. The quotas, based on the 1920 U.S. census, resulted in inordinate numbers of immigrants admitted from countries like Britain and France, and virtually no one from countries in the Asia–Pacific triangle. In 1952 immigration law was recodified, but those racist provisions of the act were carried forward in the cold war and restrictionist climate of the time and enacted over President Truman's veto. Truman didn't give up, however, and appointed a presidential commission, which responded, in 1954, with a report that became an important thread in the nascent civil rights movement.

In the Senate, action on the commission's report, and reforms proposed by President Kennedy, were locked up by judiciary chairman James O. Eastland, Democrat of Mississippi, who had neither incentive nor desire to do anything progressive about immigration. Lyndon Johnson in turn resubmitted President Kennedy's reform. In 1965, Eastland relented under the burgeoning pressure for reform; he allowed the younger brother of the deceased president to manage the bill on the Senate floor. A key provision of the bill eliminated the national-origin quotas by putting the admission of immigrants from all countries on an equal basis.

Although the bill passed, further proposals for reform were stalled; from 1965 to 1975 there was not a single meeting of the Senate subcommittee on immigration that Eastland chaired, and not one piece of legislation on general immigration policy moved through Congress.

In 1978 Eastland announced his retirement, effective at the end of the year. Teddy Kennedy, looking ahead to a judiciary committee without the southern czar, was keeping an eye on a bill on immigration policy coming over from the House, which would create a high-level commission to review immigration reforms. He had the bill "held at the desk," a device designed to avoid referring the legislation to committee, on the theory that the legislation will then be available for floor consideration. Unanimous consent is required both to hold a bill at the desk and to release it. With this tactic, Kennedy circumvented the committee and shepherded it through the Senate. President Carter signed it. Part of the bill included a provision for a 16-member select commission to study the problem of immigration. It was to include four cabinet members; four House members; four members appointed by the president from among the general public; and four members of the Senate. Kennedy, of course, was one, and he was joined by Dennis De Concini of Arizona.

Since this was to be a bipartisan commission, and the House had picked two Democrats and two Republicans, Kennedy waited for ranking Republican judiciary committee member Strom Thurmond to appoint his two. Charles Mathias of Maryland expressed an immediate interest; the problem came after that. Thurmond told Kennedy he should just choose another Democrat because there didn't seem to be another Republican interested. Kennedy, afraid that if the Senate balance was 3 to 1 the commission's bipartisanship might be endangered, asked Thurmond to try again. Thurmond went down the Republican ranks, asking member after member, and then finally latched onto newcomer Alan Simpson, the most junior Republican senator on the committee. Thurmond ushered Simpson into his office one day and congratulated him for being appointed to a new commission on immigration; before the rookie realized it, he was part of the new team.

Simpson's braintrust on immigration is headed by the staff

director of the immigration subcommittee, Richard Day. Theirs had been perhaps the most important of Simpson's working relationships on the Hill, and the way they work together illustrates how senators rely on key staff members when dealing with such blockbuster subjects as immigration.

Even when he first became involved with the immigration issue, Simpson realized he would need help with it. He decided to call on an old friend back home in Wyoming, who was at the time a partner in a law firm. Feeling a little lost and uncertain, Simpson asked Day if he'd consider transplanting himself to Washington to work for him. For Day, as it had been and would be for many others, the call from Washington was something to view with both pleasure and skepticism. An honor to be asked, and needed, yes—but one that could prove costly to the honoree. Though money was not a major factor in his mind, Day asked how much the Senate was paying the best and/or brightest to lure them to Washington; when Simpson quoted something in the $40,000 range—at that time the limit on what staff could make—Day politely declined. Even Simpson knew that 40 grand was paltry temptation for a man with a successful law practice.

After the 1980 elections, and the Republican takeover of Washington, Simpson made another call to Day—to tell him that, now, things were different. As part of the majority, for a change, Republicans would be able to lead things rather than fight them. Day said, in effect, "How nice for you." He still wouldn't budge. However, he did have a request to make of Simpson. He asked if he could get him two tickets to Ronald Reagan's inauguration. Simpson said the only tickets he had he was saving for his campaign treasurer and campaign manager, but when Day persisted, and made a crack about big shots forgetting their old pals, wheels began turning in Simpson's mind. Money, especially in small amounts, couldn't coax Day, but maybe some Washington razzmatazz could. He said he'd see what he could do.

Day and his wife Judy did come to Washington for Reagan's inauguration in 1981. They sat on the West Lawn of the Capitol on an uncommonly balmy January 20. Day remembers having "stars and stripes in my eyes" in the presence of all that pomp. He also admits to being inspired by Reagan's inaugural address and what struck him as ambitious plans for the country. After the ceremony, Simpson asked the couple back to his office; there may have been stars and stripes in Simpson's eyes, too. Day figured it would be the same old pitch, and to a degree it was, but Simpson put a new twist on it.

He told Day that Thurmond had asked him to take the chairmanship of the immigration and refugee policy subcommittee and that "if I've ever been involved in an area where I'm more likely to step in a pile of shit, I don't know of it. It's a political mine field, and I just don't want to keep looking over my shoulder all the time. I need somebody here I know and can trust." Simpson ended the plea with, "I'll pay you whatever I'm allowed to pay you."

For a minute Day was silent, and Simpson took it as negative. He went on to talk about those ungrateful citizens who elect members and send them to Washington, but when they need help they just get worried about how much money they can make. Actually, Day was silent because he was thinking, not because he was preparing to say no. The cut in pay would be over 50 percent, a fact aggravated by the disparity in costs of living between Cody, Wyoming, and Washington, D.C. But then he remembered the days when he and his wife each taught school for $5,000 a year.

The important fish was hooked, and Simpson reeled him in. Day called up his law partner and said he was going to take a two-year leave of absence. Another lawyer in the firm would assume his responsibilities. Mr. Day came to Washington.

Day had no experience at all in immigration policy, and even though that didn't bother Simpson, he humored Day by sending him down to talk with Emory Sneeden, who was working with Strom Thurmond. When Sneeden heard how Day had been recruited, he told Day that virtually the same thing had happened to him. When he got the call, Sneeden was a military judge from Thurmond's South Carolina who had retired as a general after 17 years on the army bench; he was then carrying around the blueprints of his dream house. Thurmond told him that Teddy Kennedy was going to break the backbone of the country with his attempts to split up the oil companies—and was Sneeden going to sit still for shenanigans like that? Sneeden told Thurmond that that was an antitrust issue and that he didn't know anything about antitrust law, that he hadn't even had a course in it in law school. Thurmond said hell, that didn't matter a hoot to him. He was looking for two things—loyalty and ability, and in that order. Presto, two more tickets to Washington: Sneeden and his wife.

Kennedy—still in a bit of shock over the loss of the Democratic majority and with it his judiciary committee chairmanship—told his legislative assistant for immigration affairs, Jerry Tinker, that he wanted him to go out of his way to help Simpson and Day, because he felt that the more they knew, the better off he would be. Kennedy had served in the Senate with the older Senator Simpson and had enjoyed working with the younger Simpson on the select commission. For Tinker's part, he welcomed the appearance of Day. Simpson's staff before Day had leaned too far to the right for Tinker.

Tinker and Day hit it off better than either might have expected. In August of 1981 they traveled together to refugee camps in Hong Kong and Thailand, and also visited the Cambodian and Laotian borders. Upon their return, they wrote and filed a joint report on the Southeast Asia trip.

Day has learned from Range that the afternoon will be spent on the immigration bill; he better have Simpson ready to move on it right after lunch. Day spends the morning rereading innumerable memoranda he has written to or received from Simpson. Simpson doesn't like merely to hear what he can just as well read off a piece of paper.

For the past month, memos have been flying. Simpson's have been dictated, hastily, to a secretary and then given to Day; this is their major mode of communication. On March

30, Day's memo to Simpson consisted primarily of two quotations from Michael Teitelbaum, an immigration expert at the Carnegie Foundation. Simpson seemed to like what he read. On April 11 he returned the memo.

To: Dick
From: AKS
Re: Immigration reform

I think those two comments of Michael Teitelbaum's are just tremendous and they are ones that I am going to etch on the top of my brain!

Day had suggested they might come in handy during Simpson's "speeches, media interviews, discussions with colleagues, etc." Among other things, Teitelbaum had stated that the future course of immigration reform debate would be "an important test of the thesis that U.S. politics is increasingly controlled by narrow special interests rather than representative of the broad public will."

An April 15 memo from Simpson urged making it clear to "union people" that legalization of immigrants would be in their best interests, and warned of administration generated figures on legalization, adding, "We better get our own set of figures on this one, Dick." Simpson's April 19 memo to Day advised that if an agreement could be reached between agricultural growers and the AFL-CIO, a copy should be leaked to a member of the *Washington Post*'s editorial staff. Also, Simpson wrote, "Be on the lookout for setting up a meeting with Frank Farhenkopf and Paul Laxalt and Pete Wilson and the attorney general. Let's set that up, please."

The April 22 memo was typed by the secretary exactly as Simpson had dictated it: "It might be well to call Alan Nelson at the INS and just say: Please don't be involved in any great activity during the time we are debating the bill. I am not trying to intrude on their operation at all but Lord sake, since we never do inquire about 'em they come up with the strangest things sometimes. Just tell them not to do anything that would hinder us or look like it was intended because sure as hell we haven't done a damned thing with them. Just kind of let him know that if you would, please." Other memos Simpson had found helpful were a briefing before a meeting with agricultural growers, and one that detailed administration lobbying efforts, pointing out that there were two new principal lobbyists for the Justice Department "this time around." With copies of these memoranda, including a list of potential amendments they will be faced with, Day goes in search of any last-minute requests from his boss.

Simpson and Day arrive at the Senate chamber at high noon, all those memos in their heads. Day is issued a special floor pass to permit him access, since he wasn't one of the regulars who enjoy free entry. At exactly 12:06, Baker calls up the bill.

As soon as Baker has finished his first sentence, Cranston addresses the chair. Baker, sensing a long delay in the offing, retreats to the cloakroom to pick majority secretary Howard Greene's brain on how he thinks the afternoon will shape up. Cranston continues. "I do not seek to obstruct or to delay for any substantial period of time Senate consideration" of the bill, he says, but he believes that deliberations should occur "only after each senator is afforded needed opportunity for full briefing."

Kennedy rises to Cranston's defense: "I think the senator is entitled to have his objections listened to, and I would hope that we could get the majority leader back in the chamber so that we can have some attention given to these concerns." Now it is up to Simpson to defend Baker. "Let me say that the majority leader is vitally concerned about this issue," Simpson says. "Everyone is well aware of the intensity and sincerity of the senator from California, and he is being heard."

After Simpson is through with his chat, Cranston suggests the absence of a quorum, otherwise known as a procedural method of waiting for something to happen. Or, in this case, waiting for something to be worked out. "Absence of a quorum" literally means there are fewer than 51 senators on the floor, but the convention in the Senate is to assume there are 51 members present unless a member takes note that there aren't. The chief reason for doing that is to fill time after a member finishes a speech and finds no one else on the floor waiting to speak. The member says, "Mr. President, I suggest the absence of a quorum," and the clerk begins to call the roll.

The next thirty minutes are spent in huddled colloquy. In the well of the Senate, Baker, Simpson, Kennedy, Cranston, and judiciary chairman Thurmond gather, along with Greene, Day, Jerry Tinker, and Range. Since Cranston's desire to delay is fueled to a large degree by the unavailability of his amendments at this stage, agreement to bring the bill up before the Senate is worked out with the proviso that, after action is completed today, the bill will not return to the floor until the week after next. That is what Baker wants anyway. He knows he would need all next week to wrestle with the budget resolution, and Simpson has told him there is no way in hell that the immigration bill can be passed today.

Baker calls off the quorum call to announce the complex time agreement that has been arrived at. As Baker calls out a list of more than two dozen amendments that comprise the agreement, Simpson is reminded of an old Wyoming adage about bear meat: "The longer you chew it, the bigger it gets." He notes that the bill, with all its amendments, is essentially the same as a bill passed in 1982 by a vote of 80 to 19. "There is not much new here," he complains.

Baker remains on the Senate floor until the immigration bill is safely under consideration by the full Senate and then, the minicrisis and housekeeping chore for the moment complete, ambles up the aisle and out the door and through the cloakroom, where he pauses to tell Howard Greene where he'll be for the next 40 minutes. He'll be at lunch. Baker takes the senators-only elevator to the senators-only dining room. It's where he goes when he just wants to eat lunch and doesn't want to participate in it as an art and science. And sport.

There is one sure way to tell when the Senate is involved in truly weighty business, and that is when a roll call vote is taken during lunch. For senators and their staffs, lunch is a ritual, one to be observed ceremoniously, not to be trifled with. The notion that lunch is something that can be skipped on a busy day doesn't exist here, as it does in most normal work situations; lunch is an event that commands respect. It is taken very seriously.

The members themselves rarely go to lunch; lunch comes to them. There is no shortage of eager lunch guests who want to visit the Hill and lobby them, or rub friendly elbows with them. And it works both ways, because senators never tire of trying to impress people. Lunch is a good time to do that. Senators have several cushy venues to choose from, the most popular being the Senate dining room in the Capitol, where the costliest entrée is generously underpriced at $6.95 and where members can bring in whatever outside guests they yearn to impress. Senator Spark Matsunaga of Hawaii is usually seated at the center table, in the company of a dozen or so constituents who wear leis around their necks and cheerfully pose for pictures with their senator.

If members want to be alone—if they have nobody to impress on a particular day, and prefer only the company of one another—they eat in the senators' private dining room, where Baker is today. It is absolutely, positively, and invariably private. Usually, senators do not prefer the company only of one another, but this is where they go if they do; woe unto the staffer who interrupts a senator in this sanctum sanctorum for anything other than urgent business—something on the order of a surprise appearance by the senator's wife. The room is spartan compared to the show-off ambiance of the Senate dining room, where a large stained-glass window depicting a valorous George Washington watches over diners.

In addition, senators can reserve one of the numerous little rooms in the Capitol to serve invited groups catered lunches prepared according to menus composed by their secretaries. This is the preferred alternative for mass impressing—delegations of 20 or more from the home state who are individually deemed insufficiently important to rate a private lunch, but whom the senator certainly does not want to ignore. They go home happy and proud and even moderately well fed. They have had lunch with the senator.

Senators have been known to leave the Hill for lunch, but not because they are lured by gourmet delicacies—unless one considers money a gourmet delicacy. For a fee, an honorarium, a senator will be lunchtime speaker at a convention or a symposium. It's a convenient way to partake of cold chicken and $2,000. The top draws can clean up at this hour; they can make more money at lunch than they do during the rest of the day. Or even the rest of the week.

Staffers, seldom in demand as public speakers, are the ones who keep Capitol Hill restaurants and their credit-card imprint machines humming at lunchtime. Denizens of the Hill virtually beg for stratification, and lunchtime has its own anthropology. Most people fall into one of a few clearly definable categories:

Deep lunch. Not for everyone, but definitely for those staffers whose lunch tab will be picked up by a lobbyist interested in a particular piece of legislation—heavyweights like Hildenbrand, Greene, Cannon, and Range. Deep lunch is worth leaving the Hill for; it's a cheap cab ride to downtown Washington where powermongers romp and dine at expense-account bistros like Duke Zeibert's, a Washington institution; Mel Krupin's, Duke's chief rival for lunch-hour heavy spenders; the Palm, so masculine it's almost brawny, and decorated comfortingly with caricatures of city movers and shakers; and a lavish array of expensive French restaurants (for the more genteel kinds of wheeling and dealing) like Maison Blanche (very near the White House, appropriately enough, and the successor in status and popularity to the now defunct Sans Souci); Le Pavilion; Le Lion d'Or; and others where the waiters have almost forgotten that American Express cards come in green as well as gold. There is no limit as to how expensive a lunch staffers can accept from a lobbyist, or how often, but generally schedules limit them to one lunch per day. Range the workaholic will go deep lunch about once a month, time permitting.

Yuppie lunch. For those still high on the excitement of working on the Hill and anxious to remain within its aura at lunchtime—people like Dodd's aides Mike Naylor and Robert Dockerty—there are a few restaurants within walking distance that have become hangouts, like on a college campus. The Chesapeake Bagel Factory on Pennsylvania Avenue is very popular, as a long line leading out the door from noon until 1:30 attests. Standing in line is part of the experience here; people talk about their condo payments, a foreign movie, or their latest time on the old 10-k run.

Other favorite hangouts are the American Café, off Massachusetts Avenue, La Brasserie, and Pendleton's, but the grand dame of this group is the Monocle, something of a landmark on the Hill and a place where staffers can be assured of running into those senators and congressmen who are not eating in the Capitol building itself. This place practically qualifies as an official extension; it's very clubby. The second floor is decorated with photographs of legislators who've frequented the place (there are several of Tip O'Neill). Some deep-lunch lobbying goes on here, but most of it is confined to the cushier restaurants downtown. After all, many staffers feel that being in the Monocle is like still being at the office, except that there are waiters and tablecloths and drinks.

Running lunch, or I'm-too-busy-for-lunch lunch. For people like Mary Jane Checchi, who insist they have no time to eat, affairs of state having become oppressively pressing, grabbing a bite is most easily accomplished at a Häagen-Dazs ice cream shop opened in 1979 on Pennsylvania Avenue, or at Bob's Ice Cream, on Massachusetts Avenue, a Washington passion whose reputation was built largely on its Oreo-cookie ice cream, widely imitated by others.

The true believers' lunch. For those who really don't want to take much time, those so hard core about their jobs that they want to work through the lunch hour, sinking their teeth into some legislative tangle as well as into some pastrami. These people—Steve Bell's secretary, on assignment, among them—dash down to the carry-out shop where Betty and Virginia dole out sandwiches wrapped in wax paper or the daily special, which tends to taste better than it looks, then dash back to their desks and work.

This particular breed can also make use of the Senate cafeteria, a return to the good-old-days of cafeterianism. Almost large enough to be cavernous, it occupies most of the basement of the Dirksen building. While technically closed to the public from 11:30 until 1:00 P.M., this is a rule that is usually bent or broken. There is a sandwich line and a hot meal line, both of them offering Senate bean soup and cornbread, specialties of the house—or, rather, of the Senate. In the cafeteria one finds many lunchers who truly just want to be left alone: who don't want their lapels creased by interested parties or to gnaw over the rigors of the day. They might as well wear buttons that say, "Don't bother me, I'm eating." But they prefer staying in the cafeteria to using the carryout line and returning to the office because, unless they are in high-command positions, they know that if they're in the office they are expected to work, sandwich in hand or no. In the cafeteria they are fairly safe from the ring of the dread telephone.

Following his own lunch, and another meeting with TV executives, Frank Lautenberg sits down with Checchi and his legislative director Eve Lubalin for a legislative briefing session. Although immigration is the subject Lautenberg will be dealing with when he gets to the floor this afternoon, the procedure surrounding the bill is centerstage in Checchi's mind. Lautenberg has never served in the House; he is busy getting used to the Senate. But Checchi sees immigration as a prime example, tremendously useful for pedagogical purposes, of how one chamber can influence the course of action in the other.

Federalist number 63 supports an oft quoted (probably aprocyphal) story involving George Washington and Thomas Jefferson in which Jefferson explains that he pours coffee from his cup into his saucer to cool it, and Washington says, "We pour legislation into the senatorial saucer to cool it." Washington's supposition was derived from the basic differences in design between the two chambers, and by the belief on the part of the founders that the two chambers should be separate political entities, the House theoretically basing its actions more on popular opinion and the Senate correcting the House on the basis of its (assumed) maturity and experience.

The difference in size would account for the chief distinction between the House and the Senate: the original projection, which prevailed for nearly 200 years, was that the House would require strict discipline, authoritatively or oligarchically, lest it sink into anarchic futility. The Senate, on the other hand, would be a chamber where individualism was tempered by deference to the collective wisdom of the body. The House would be a legislation machine, the Senate, a debating chamber or national sounding board.

To keep House members more oriented toward individualistic functions of representation, the length of term was set at two years, fostering the desire for productivity, increasing the instability of the job, and encouraging contact with citizens back home. The House became more formal in its proceedings, with power less evenly distributed, and legislative action was dispensed with more quickly once it got to the floor. Meanwhile, the Senate, with fewer rules, had greater flexibility and was more informal.

Not surprisingly, the result was that individual outlooks between House members and senators varied significantly. No longer. During the last decade, the two chambers have become more and more like each other, with chores that were formerly done by one chamber now being performed rather ineffectively by the other.

The House has become more like the Senate for several reasons. One is that the House leadership has lost firm control over its schedule. There are now more individuals holding important positions; hence the leadership positions mean less. In addition, House members, largely because they have admitted television cameras into the chamber, and because House proceedings can be seen nationwide on cable TV, are becoming better known than their predecessors. And better known in some cases than many senators.

The Senate is beginning to look like the House because it is less leisurely, less personal, more formal, more organized, and more centered around perpetual campaigning than it used to be. By relying more and more on staff, and less on traditional rules and procedure, the Senate has moved itself away from being a debating society and closer to the daily legislative grind of the House.

Standing rules of the Senate are supposed to encourage thoughtful deliberation rather than speed, and devolve power on the individual instead of on the majority. The rules are anchored firmly in the history of the Senate. Unlike the House rules, which are adopted anew every two years, the Senate's standing rules remain in force and are seldom changed, even though virtually every member complains about them. When they are changed, it is usually the result of painful compromise, rather than majority fiat. Indeed, 16 of the Senate's original 20 rules have substantially survived to this day.

Yet very few members of the Senate community, including the senators themselves, ever take the trouble to understand the rules, their nuances and implications. The two biggest results of this are that there is always an enormous amount of misinformation being circulated about Senate procedure, and that those few individuals who do know what they are talking about when it comes to the standing rules and parliamentary ploys are much in demand and take on an almost mythic presence.

When Martin Gold, Baker's former procedural expert, was still in the Senate, walking through the Capitol with him was like walking with a member: senators would stop him in the halls asking for consultations and recommendations, reporters would ask him for help in deciphering what was being played out on the Senate floor, and of course other staffers would be tracking him down to pick his brain so they could impress their bosses with a strategy or get a step up on the opposition. Baker was proud of his specialist, and would freely offer Gold's services to other Republican senators when they found themselves tied up in a procedural knot.

The ability of the modern Senate to do its business with eighteenth-century rules is a tribute to accommodation and compromise, but also helps explain the Senate's problems of stagnation and frustration. The modern Senate has never struck a comfortable balance between the role of the institution and the powers of the individual.

If observed to the letter, the rules would soon become an unacceptable albatross for the Senate to bear. Frequently, they are circumvented by unanimous consent. Nevertheless, the need to secure such consent in order to operate demonstrates the power of individual members and the need to accommodate their interests whenever possible. At the same time, individuals are careful not to abuse this power, knowing that with the abuse comes legislative paralysis and rejections for favors later on. The fact that many senators are now asserting their individual prerogatives more than ever before has led to the widespread view that recent changes in Senate procedure have tipped the balance more toward the individual, and away from the institution.

The heart and center of Senate procedure lies in the power of the individual and in the guaranteed rights of the minority. Senate rules remain a great reservoir of individual prerogatives. Often, this has proven a bane to a Senate majority seeking to act upon its legislative agenda. Over the years many proposals have been circulated to promote greater efficiency and majoritarian rule. Yet, the general consensus has been that these adjustments may have destroyed the character of the institution. Rather than changing its rules to sap individual power, the Senate has preferred to take the riskier but more crowd-pleasing course of accommodation.

The filibuster rule is a case in point. In many legislative bodies, it is possible for a simple majority to "move the previous question" and abruptly terminate debate. Such a motion exists today in the House, and was part of the first Senate rules. In the Senate it was seldom if ever used, and by 1806 it was dropped altogether.

From that time until World War I, there existed no mechanism in the Senate to close debate. This fact enabled a group of isolationist senators to filibuster to death President Wilson's bill to arm merchant ships. Wilson railed against the "little band of willful men" and a consensus developed that the balance between individual rights and institutional needs had to be recast.

The remedy was cloture, a procedure which requires a supermajority vote and which sets into motion procedures for a gradual termination of leave. Still, cloture is several steps removed from a motion for the previous question. Two days must elapse from the time a cloture motion is made to the moment the vote on cloture occurs. More than a simple majority is needed to impose it, and achieving cloture does not in itself end debate. Up to 100 hours can remain of debate even after cloture is achieved.

Thus, cloture is a compromise of sorts. The institution requires a timely means of considering legislation. The individual desires the capacity to be heard and to slow, if not halt, the legislative juggernaut. Cloture achieves these purposes consistent with the Senate's deliberative constitutional role, but cloture is cumbersome. At first, the rule required a two-thirds vote of *all* senators to be invoked. In the absence of cloture, individual prerogatives were essentially unfettered. Today the rule has been loosened, but a three-fifths vote is still needed. Without it, a filibuster, even by a single individual, can stop legislation in its tracks.

Even with a cloture procedure available to wind down filibusters, the potential for individual power is still impressive, particularly at the end of a yearly session. In the mid-seventies Senator James Allen of Alabama blocked many legislative measures by the mere threat of a filibuster. Often, the time remaining before adjournment was too compressed and the list of remaining bills too long for the Senate leadership to meet each threat with cloture, so only the most essential bills went through. Effectively, the powers rooted in the Senate's eighteenth-century rules enabled Allen to determine end-of-session agendas. While he could not decide what measures would be called up, or do more than anyone else to enact legislation, he in effect decided what bills would not pass and in most cases prevailed.

In the eighties, Allen's role has been assumed by Howard Metzenbaum, whose ideology and negative agenda are distinct from Allen's but whose tactics are similar. During the last month of session, when the calendar is crowded and floor time is at a premium, Metzenbaum polices the Senate floor, armed with a list of bills to which he will object. Faced with having to use time-consuming procedures to defeat Metzenbaum's tactics, Baker has, more often than he would like, been forced to pass only the less controversial end-of-session measures.

On the Senate floor, all ears have turned to Republican Steven Symms of Idaho, who has embarked on a rambling, extensive attack on Republican Charles Grassley of Iowa. Some on the floor, including Simpson, are mystified as to why Symms is going to such lengths to attack a fellow conservative. Gradually, those who have been listening to Symms speak, and those who have likely hurried in from the cloakroom to catch this particular act, get the impression that the senator may be inebriated. The word in the cloakroom is that Symms had taken his secretaries out to celebrate Secretaries Week and lingered too long at lunch. When he finally sits down, the chamber sighs in relief.

Baker enters the chamber and gives a deep sigh. Howard Greene has filled him in on Symms, and has stated that the two cloakrooms have finished working out the details of the time agreement on the immigration bill. Baker receives recognition from the presiding officer, and after putting in an order that the Senate will stand in recess following today's business until noon on Monday, begins to recite the unanimous consent agreement from the cloakrooms. Once again, Symms speaks up. "I somehow wonder if the country is aware," he says, "that we are talking about, in this bill to allow everything that has happened with respect to crossing our borders in immigration, to say that everything that happened in the past is OK, but any of you people out there, you small businessmen or farmers, who hire any illegal aliens, we are going to arrest you."

Baker doesn't quite understand what Symms is attempting to do, but since he is on the floor to push through a unanimous consent agreement that one member alone can ruin, he decides to be patient. The two go back and forth for a while, Baker pleading that "this opportunity to deal with this matter on a well-organized basis" shouldn't be thrown away.

SYMMS: Mr. President, I make a point of order that a quorum is not present.
BYRD: The senator does not have the floor.
THE PRESIDING OFFICER: The majority leader has the floor.
SYMMS: Mr. President, I reserve the right to object. I make a point of order that a quorum is not present.
BYRD: The senator cannot make that point of order without having the floor.
BAKER: I am willing for the senator to do that. . . . I have no desire to interfere with the senator's wishes. Agreements of this sort are perishable and amendments grow like mushrooms. If we let this thing grow much larger, there will be so many mushrooms on it we will never get it through.

Following that plea, Baker changes the time slated for voting on the bill the week after next from 4:00 to 2:00. This is enough to silence Symms.

Simpson takes a deep breath; years of work in the unglamorous realm of immigration reform are once again looking like they will bear fruit.

Kennedy has placed two amendments before the Senate on this first day of consideration of the immigration bill. Simpson doesn't like either of them. The first would "sunset" the bill's employer sanction provisions. "Sunsetting" means that the provisions would expire on a specific date unless they were reaffirmed beforehand. The second amendment would extend by two years the date by which an alien who entered the United States could qualify for temporary residence status. Kennedy loses on both, as Republican unity rates are 75 percent and 94 percent, respectively, while the Democrats are 68 percent and 56 percent.

Just as Frank Lautenberg is getting ready to sit down with yet another group of broadcasters, this one from WCAU-TV of Philadelphia, the bells ring to signal a vote on the first of the Kennedy amendments. There is no way to plan such meetings so they won't be disturbed by a vote, and many times votes break up meetings and devastate afternoons. If a staff has arranged four back-to-back meetings of 15 minutes each in an afternoon, and the bells ring signifying a vote, the senator will then leave for the 15-minute subway trip to and from the office to the Capitol. Perhaps he then gets stopped by a colleague on the floor who wants a favor. His entire afternoon schedule can be pushed back an hour or more. Lautenberg isn't accustomed to this kind of uncertainty.

Meanwhile, Steve Bell and Pete Domenici have spent most of today's session pleading for compromise with the Republican budget working group. But the meeting has gone nowhere. Back on the floor, Bell quietly asks Domenici if he has delivered the bad news to Baker. Domenici says no, but he is about to. Bell is not in good humor. He has heard that Domenici's Democratic counterpart on the budget committee, Lawton Chiles, has gone wild-turkey hunting in the Virginia countryside this morning (literally—this is not one of Jim Range's metaphors). It just didn't seem fair to Bell. Here they are in the majority at last—after all these years—with a president of their own party, and Chiles has gone hunting. Victorious over the budget committee once already, Chiles is more than content to let things continue that way when the bill comes up on Monday.

Shortly before 5:00, with the voting on a Kennedy amendment just over, Baker takes advantage of the fact that most of the members are still on the floor to announce the schedule for the rest of the day. Members may ignore each other's speeches most of the time, but they do listen to Baker when he talks about the schedule. They are interested in basically one thing at this point: will there be any more votes today? When Baker tells them there won't be, it is the signal to bolt, like the bell going off in junior high school. Baker, who has it in mind to take off early tonight so he can attend a reception James Sasser of Tennessee is holding for the Memphis Blues—a reception that a large number of Tennesseeans will be attending—keeps to the plan.

Nearly two hours later, with Baker long gone, Ted Stevens is coping with the duty of closing the Senate down, essentially mundane housekeeping details. For 45 minutes, the Senate has been conducting "morning business," and today, as on most days, there are a wide variety of submissions. Charles Mathias of Maryland introduces a bill to "authorize the casting of the reverse of the Great Seal of the United States"; Danforth, a bill titled, "The Construction Contract Payment Procedures Act of 1983," which he says will "inject some basic common sense into the government's current practices regarding retainage on its construction contracts"; Lowell Weicker of Connecticut, Mack Mattingly of Georgia, and Sam Nunn of Georgia have earlier submitted statements in support of the contracts measures; Mark Andrews of North Dakota appears in person to deliver a speech requesting that the select committee on Indian affairs become a permanent committee of the Senate; William Armstrong of Colorado drops in to discuss Soviet prison camps; Kennedy has earlier submitted a bill on behalf of himself and seven others that provides for health care for unemployed workers; Armstrong offers a prepared statement on "The Truth about Vietnam," including several articles on the subject which will fill 12 pages of the record; Jesse Helms of North Carolina enters into the record an article on abortion and the conscience of the

165

nation by R. Reagan, which he has read in the current issue of the *Human Life Review* and which Helms insists deserves "close review"; Chiles, back from his turkey hunt, submits a prepared statement on Child Abuse Month. And so on.

Elizabeth Baldwin, who works for Howard Greene in the cloakroom, and who is in charge of closing, has a file handy with all the "shopkeeping" requests to be addressed before the Senate goes out. Ted Stevens waits for Robert Byrd to arrive on the floor, and the two of them—alone except for the ever-present staff and a handful of onlookers in the gallery—do the nitty-gritty work. At 7:12 H. John Heinz of Pennsylvania bangs the gavel, which brings the day to an official close.

Since the Senate will not be in session on Friday, and much of the committee work will be limited to expendable and perfunctory sessions, members are essentially free to leave the city—and do they ever. Easterners are already on the way home; their cars clog the special congressional-perk parking spaces right next to the terminals at nearby National Airport. Most of the westerners spend the night in Washington, and catch late-morning flights back home, unless they are so desperate to get out that they are willing to brave a red-eye.

Simpson, who has spent the previous hour going over events with Richard Day, feels relieved. He has surmounted one hurdle without too much pain, and now has some time to gear himself up for the real battles that will take place when the bill reappears. That, however, will not happen for more than a week, and lobbying groups, colleagues, and the press will make the most of the days in between.

With the prospect of relative peace ahead of him, measurable though it is in hours rather than days, Simpson will not agonize over Senate business tonight. He will take his wife out to dinner—seeking sanctuary and momentarily finding it.

5

~⚬~

FRIDAY AND BEYOND

My wife says to me, "If you were really out there doing some-
thing important, if I thought you were able to do something
for the country, I wouldn't mind the time you were away from
me and the family. But if I think that you are out there an-
swering quorum calls and listening to someone go on about
some tiny unimportant amendment, it's not worth it."

DAVID BOREN (D-OKLA.)

Awakening on a blessed Friday during which the Senate
will not be in session, senators and their staffs who are still in
Washington hasten to plot avenues of escape. For Baker and
Simpson, it will be a day away from the capital—but hardly
away from politics. They and more than a dozen of their colleagues are making preparations for a big trip to Houston and
a salute to John Tower, who will be feted at the kind of oversized fundraiser peculiar, like so many oversized things, to
Texas.

At noon, Dodd will be flying down to Miami to make a
speaking appearance before the United Jewish Appeal of Florida; he's still flush with what he considered his television vic-

tory of Wednesday night. Checchi, most of her lessons for Lautenberg now behind her, is thinking not just about leaving the Senate for the week, but about leaving it for good. She remembers she thought she had left it for good before. But visions of the novel she just knows she can write return and begin dancing in her head.

Few members show up at the office, and those who do feel a little like kids in school on a Saturday. With the ambiance cooler and less formal, most staff members let their usual manic industriousness relent, at least a little. Some show up in sloppy khakis and Lacoste shirts, eschewing the usual tie and suits. Nearly everyone takes it easy.

But not, of course, Steve Bell. He is as button-down and buttoned-up as ever, arriving at the office in full workday regalia and summoning his senior staff in for a meeting behind a firmly closed door. He is determined to use the free day for still more wrestling with the budget, which he imagines himself on the verge of overpowering with a brilliantly administered headlock. He has only this weekend to get his committee's act together, and he is still riddled with doubt about whether his side will win and what the budget resolution will look like when all the grappling is over.

And then there is Range. Dressed in baggy jeans, chain-smoking his way through the corridors, he is going to spend at least part of the day staring what he considers to be a personal setback squarely in the face. Today, staff on the environment and public works committee begin preparing hearings on the nomination of William Ruckelshaus for the job of EPA administrator. Range had wanted that baby for himself, wanted it with a passion, knew he was the right man for it, wouldn't have minded kissing the majority leader's office goodbye, for all the respect and esteem he lavished on Baker. To keep his morale up, and take his mind off bad news, he interrupts himself at irregular intervals throughout the day and rushes outside to the old beat-up yellow pickup truck he has parked out in front of the Capitol, because there waiting for him is his beloved old dog Jambo, a sleek black labrador retriever. Range plays with him and feeds him and takes him for walks around the grounds. He often brings Jambo in with him, for his own benefit as much as the dog's. Jambo has a knack for cheering him up.

The environment and public works committee has been consumed in Ruckelshaus talk all week, and that will continue this morning. Yesterday, Reagan had formally sent the nomination of Ruckelshaus up to the Senate, thereby shifting the focus away from Ann Burford, whose resignation had been juicy—indeed, sloppy—news for weeks. Range feels a keen territorial interest in the proceedings, not only because he has harbored hopes of getting Burford's job himself; environment and public works is "his" old committee, and the environment dearest to his heart of all issues he has dealt with. As Baker's assistant on the committee, Range played a key role in the writing and passing of Superfund legislation and the clean air and clean water acts. Since those glory days, Baker has rarely appeared at the committee's meetings, so Range, and Baker legislative assistant Jo Cooper, play Baker's role for him. Range is known as the kind of guy who can get more agitated over threats to an eagle sanctuary or a snail darter than over the threat of nuclear war.

Baker knows all this. After discussing it with Range, and after Burford's resignation, he had put in a call to White House chief of staff Jim Baker suggesting Range for the post. Some thought that Range, at 36, was too young and too inexperienced as a manager for such a position. Others felt his knowledge of the environment and his senatorial savoir-faire would overshadow any shortcomings. Response to Baker's suggestion was also mixed at the 9:30 meetings. James Cannon, for one, wasn't crazy about the idea, and Tommy Griscom privately worried about Baker committing himself and his office too heavily to something that might have no chance. Everyone, though, had given Range "go-get-'em" verbal support on the day he went to the White House to be interviewed for the job.

The way the Ruckelshaus nomination was handled is a reflection on how the environment committee has been operating under Republican control. Committee members were pleased and relieved to hear that Ruckelshaus had been nominated; they liked him, and he seemed so clearly a step up from the surly and unpopular Burford.

The idea of putting committee chairman Robert Stafford in the awkward position of taking on the White House over the nomination certainly does not appeal to them but, even so, committee members don't want to make it too easy for an administration they feel has been weak on environmental issues (and has paid too little attention to the work of the committee). Thus though it had become clear that Ruckelshaus, and certainly not Range, is the nominee, plans have been afoot to "dirty up" Ruckelshaus' name as a strategic procedural ploy. Committee members want to show those in the environmental activist community that the committee is still fighting for their interests, and they want the White House to know that the committee is not to be taken for granted. So the committee has decided to let the environmentalists testify *before* Ruckelshaus—an unusual procedure for a nominee and a not-so-subtle way of making him uneasy and intimidating him. Through their testimony, the leaders and groups will be able to tell the committee what they expect of the new nominee.

Even though Range is unhappy that he has not been chosen for the job, he doesn't like the way the committee is approaching the Ruckelshaus nomination. He thinks committee members are "screwing up," making themselves look ridiculous. He doesn't have much patience with petty politics.

In the 1970s, when the environment was a hot issue in Congress, things were different. Members were eager to get involved. When Range was a staffer on the environment and public works committee in the halcyon days of the movement—when the issues were broad and simple, as clear as clean water—he helped shepherd through some of the groundbreaking environmental legislation. But he always felt not enough was being done. Who indeed would have wanted to come out against clean water, or clean air? It was the greening of Congress in a way, the "Happy Days" of the environmental movement and the legislators who wanted to be identified with it. Baker and Muskie dominated the committee in a spirit of virtually festive bipartisan cooperation.

Then Baker reached the point at which he thought he'd done his share of humble service to the earth; it was now someone else's turn. He had been there for the heyday and, conveniently enough, would be escaping before things turned sour. He would continue, with Range's assistance, to establish minimum standards on important legislation, but he never got involved in the way that he had before.

His timing was perfect, and so was Muskie's; the latter backed off the environment and devoted himself more to the budget committee. Environmental law and the environmental litigation that goes with it became one of the most complicated aspects in all of law and legislation. Somehow, along the way, the romance and the passion of the movement were replaced by the mundane pedantics of litigation. What was once a merry realm of earth days and balloons had moved indoors to the courtroom. Members had to consider not only ecological factors, but also how legislation and regulation would affect the economy, their own regions, and the voters who lived there.

In the late seventies, with chairman Jennings Randolph, Democrat of West Virginia, getting older and less influential, Stafford, despite the fact that he was a Republican, became a darling of the environmentalists. But when Stafford became chairman, the attitude changed; the love affair was over. Randolph had been successful as a chairman because he was willing to go along with the consensus of the committee, rather than holding out for his own pet projects. He compromised even on issues about which he felt strongly. Baker and Muskie got most of the credit, but Randolph provided foresight and ingenuity and helped make the committee efficient.

Stafford, a nice quiet man from Vermont, was not considered a born leader, and the staff of his committee enjoyed no great support in the Senate. He had said on more than one occasion that he didn't want to run for reelection in 1982; he was talked into it by Baker and others, who promised that he wouldn't get any opposition from the Republican party's strong right wing. The national environmental groups actually helped Stafford in his reelection, a favor he didn't forget. The environmentalists and his staff considered him one of the last holdouts for the environmental community in the Republican ranks of the Senate. But the perception was a bit different in the Senate itself.

As one environmentalist said, reflecting on Stafford's stewardship, "The committee just crumbled." Issues like toxic waste dumps and acid rain, highly charged and volatile, got nowhere in the committee; inflexibility on both sides led to stalemate. As a result, most important legislation had been moved by the environmental pollution subcommittee chairman John Chafee of Rhode Island. He passed and delivered on a barrier islands treaty, which cut off federal aid to the barrier islands, thus ending harmful construction there; the endangered species act, which prohibited federal agencies from carrying out projects threatening the habitats of endangered species; and the clean water act, which makes it unlawful to discharge "dredged or fill material" into a waterway. It was the force of Chafee's personality, coupled with the best balancing act in the Senate between environmental and industry concerns, that enabled him to get such things done. The problem was that much of this legislation lost its way once it got to Stafford's full committee. It ended up in limbo, that legislative twilight zone that harbors so many best-laid plans.

Chafee took little joy from his subcommittee's small victories. The lack of cooperation in the Senate disillusioned him. He has said, "There is very little fellowship in the Senate. What I think of the Senate is: My grandfather had a farm when we were growing up. They'd let the cows out in the morning, and then, around feeding time, the cows would all come in close to the paddock, and then the farmer would open the door and the cows would come in and they all knew their own stanchions; they'd move down the separate alleys in the barn and head for their stanchion, put their head in, and eat their hay and grain. And that's what the Senate reminds me of. You go over to vote, you come back to your office, put your head in the stanchion again. There's very little camaraderie, I find."

Chafee's sense of disillusion is hardly unique. For senators, the disappointments of life in the Senate can be more than professional; they can be intensely, and dramatically, personal. The new arrivals expect the Senate to change their lives. It can change them in ways they would not have expected and never have wanted.

It's The Syndrome. It goes like this:

Ambition. Desire. Confidence. Faith. Commitment. Struggle. Sacrifice. Self-assertion. Conflict. Victory. Goals, ideals, agendas, plans, vision. Washington. Realization. Repudiation. Compromise. Frustration, disillusion, revision, reversion. Apathy. Indifference. Futility. Regret.

It is bad enough for a new member to discover, in running the course, that the United States Senate is hardly the powerful paradise he has imagined; it is worse, sometimes even traumatic, when these babes from outlying woods learn that their personal lives may become not more satisfying and more glamorous, but in fact less satisfying, unglamorous, even an ordeal. A smart arrival will be able to perceive within his first 60 days that the place is not filled with geniuses and nobles, that the institution does not function like a well-oiled machine, and that one member will most likely not have the dramatic impact on the affairs of the nation, or on the conduct of the Senate, that he might have thought.

They aren't all naive Mr. and Ms. Smiths, of course—hopping off trains at Union Station and rushing to catch a glimpse of the Capitol. In fact, Union Station has been a hideous bureaucratic debacle for years, and remains a symbolic eyesore on which millions have been squandered by Congress (another new version of it is supposed to open in 1986), and the Capitol itself is badly in need of repair and the object of agitated congressional debate. But even if they don't touch down at National Airport expecting an inspiring display of democracy in action, they do come here, usually, with their own lofty preconceptions and a few ideals that have not been thrashed or abandoned. They will learn that the reality of the Senate is as hostile to that kind of attitude as the idea of the Senate is conducive to it.

For even the smartest, savviest, and least romantic newcomer, there is a rude awakening. What he or she will learn is that the Senate can come between the member and the family whose tolerance and encouragement presumably helped him or her get there. The Senate forces family into the background, disrupting—in extreme cases even destroying—normal family life. The Senate can be an all-consuming homewrecker, one that has indeed wrecked many homes.

Normally, it takes a while for a senator to realize what a negative force the Senate can be on one's domestic life. Not so for Warren Rudman, Republican of New Hampshire. For Rudman, the news came in a bulletin, swift and to the point. When he was elected to the Senate in 1980, his wife Shirley told him, in effect, "Congratulations—have a nice trip." Rudman soon found himself living alone in a small apartment near the Capitol and attending mandatory social gatherings stag. His wife and three children stayed behind, cozy and comfortable, in the family's spacious Nashua, New Hampshire, house. Rudman became a Senate widower virtually overnight. In a way, he was fortunate. His marriage survived even if he can only reach out and touch his wife by phone. Also, the bad news came quickly; other senators' marriages suffered only a gradual decay, like the West Front of the Capitol. Malcolm Wallop was divorced after five years in the Senate. Lowell Weicker was divorced after seven years in the Senate.

And Chris Dodd, the ambitious young Democrat, the aspiring spokesman for his party, was divorced while still in his first year in the Senate.

The Senate makes a testy mistress. The toll on family life is exacted by the demands the Senate makes on its members; they must attend to everyone who stakes claims to their time, their attention, their votes. Family demands come second, so dinners are missed, birthdays are missed, graduations are missed, even funerals are missed. Vacations are arranged according to Senate schedules instead of the family's wishes, and may have to be postponed or abandoned even so. If a senator speaks to his wife at 4:00 P.M. and tells her the Senate will recess in a couple of hours and dinner should be scheduled for 7:00, and then at 6:00 the head of a PAC that gave generously to his last campaign calls to say he'd like to drop by the office in an hour for a little chat, nine times out of ten dinner will have to wait, wife and family with it.

Howard Baker once had to write a letter to Kevin Cohen, son of William Cohen of Maine, explaining to the young man why his father had to miss his college awards ceremony: because Baker needed Cohen on the floor for a critical vote. It happens all the time. The cumulative effect on a marriage and a family can be severe. Many members contend that they don't let their families bear the burdens of office, but it's almost impossible not to. The very fact that while in Washington they will be separated from their real homes makes it so.

Usually, one person more than any other suffers from this situation: the senator's wife. Senators' wives are an oppressed minority.

Joy Baker is not a typical Senate wife by any means, but she represents an extreme that is symptomatic of the pressures and demands of political patriarchies. She will not be joining her husband for the political trip to Texas to stroke John Tower's ego, but there have been and will be numerous other events during the year that she does attend, no matter how much she prefers to be elsewhere. Political daughter turned political wife, she understands. The only child of Everett McKinley Dirksen, long-time Senate kingfish, Joy Baker had excessive exposure to politics long before she said yes to the ambitious young politico from Tennessee, himself a product of a congressional family. She knew what was in store for her—the difficulties of raising a family virtually on her own, the tensions that come with having an absentee husband who is also wedded to a senatorial career—but awareness is not always protection. Her long-running battle with alcoholism was for years one of Washington's worst-kept secrets; many even speculated that it was to blame when Gerald R. Ford failed to pick Howard Baker as his running mate in 1976.

Mrs. Baker recovered from alcoholism, but has remained plagued by misfortune. Since her husband became majority leader, Mrs. Baker has constantly been in and out of hospitals. She had a portion of her stomach removed; three ribs were removed; and she broke her left knee tripping over a telephone cord in the middle of the night. When she entered the hospital for treatment of lung cancer, and had a portion of a lung removed, Senator Baker was shocked, even panicked. In the midst of his concern, he recalled that she'd told him she had always wanted a Jaguar. Released from the hospital, she was picked up by her husband in the new Jaguar he had bought her as a gift.

One consequence of all the travail was that some people in Washington felt sorry for Howard Baker and what they viewed as an added burden for him. Stories abound of Mrs. Baker's refusals to go on some scheduled trips, canceling dinner appearances, and phoning the office and insisting on speaking to her husband at inappropriate times, like in the middle of a critical vote. Many such tales are true, despite the fact that Baker even employs a female staff person assigned the task of taking care of the woman whom they call "Mrs. B" and whom Howard Baker affectionately calls "mom."

But Joy Baker has invaluable assets as well as liabilities. She is considered by really knowledgeable insiders to be extremely intelligent politically, blessed with an impeccable memory for faces, names, events, everything, and instincts about the individuals surrounding her husband that are perhaps even keener than his own. Such practicalities aside, everyone knows Howard Baker is tremendously devoted to his wife. He dotes on her. His face really does light up when he walks into the office to find her there.

Baker's is not the only Senate family to have been touched by alcoholism. Of his peers, at least five are considered alcoholics by Hill insiders; it is likely there are more. Their bouts with the bottle are rarely reported in the press; for one thing, there is so much social drinking in Washington that it's hard to tell the professionals from the seasoned amateurs. For another, the Senate "club" system tends to close ranks around those members whose drinking problems have the potential to become embarrassing.

Washington undoubtedly has the highest per capita consumption of liquor of any city in the country. Social drinking is a major indoor sport, especially for politicos. If a senator is scheduled to attend three functions in one night, it is likely he or she will be handed a drink upon arriving at each. To refuse would be indecorous; it would be like turning down some ethnic delicacy during a campaign tour. There is more pressure to eat, drink, and be merry than to exercise prudence or temperance.

As for the Senate protecting its own, there have been incidents in recent years of senators and staff members joining to escort a tipsy member safely off the floor and back to the Marble Room, a private chamber off the Senate floor that has seen its share of basket cases. Capitol policemen take it as one of their duties to play clandestine nursemaid to the occasional senator who totters into the Capitol late at night after an evening of overindulgence. Since many of the male senators are wifeless in Washington, there's no one else to pick up the pieces and put them back together.

A few senators are known for their public displays of physical fitness—William Proxmire is a seemingly tireless jogger, John Heinz takes his tennis seriously, John Warner rushes out at lunchtime to play racquetball—and the members do have a gymnasium at their disposal, their own private health club, to help them stay in shape. But, by and large, they do not take care of themselves. The officers of the average large American corporation probably have much better health and exercise habits. Senators work long hours, overeat, overdrink, oversmoke, and—ambitious, impatient, and aggressive as they tend to be—push themselves to the limit in a high-stress environment. Those who haven't already had them are like heart attacks waiting to happen.

Most of the time, they tend not to take this possibility seriously. After Dr. Freeman Carey, the Capitol physician, finished extolling the virtues of physical activity to a group of senators and left for other business, one of the senators cracked that his idea of "working out" was watching Jane Fonda's exercise tape—from his favorite living-room easy chair. Occasionally, though, senators are forced to think about the bodies they are mistreating. When secretary of the Senate William Hildenbrand returned to the Senate sporting the scars of a triple bypass, senators queried him anxiously, and at length, about his operation and the symptoms that preceded it, not only out of their interest in him but also out of their interest in themselves. Too easily, many could picture themselves in the same situation.

His health is one thing Howard Baker is not worried about on this particular Friday. After all, he is still cherishing the "no ulcer" findings of doctors from the previous weekend as if they were a gold star given him by the Lord. Nor is he dreading the trip to Texas, as he might. It is one of those professional duties he has long since learned how to handle painlessly. His neatly typed itinerary from scheduler Lisa Baker (no relation) tells him exactly where he is supposed to be when, and just like it says, at 11:45 A.M., he arrives at Andrews Air Force Base where no less an airplane than Air Force One is waiting to take him, Ronald Reagan, and the usual presidential retinue to Texas. As a friendly gesture, Reagan has invited Baker to fly with him.

Baker's Capitol office is, save for Range and his assistant, Mary Kay O'Hara, quiet for the day. But his other office, in the Hart building, is still churning away. One of its principal occupations is, indeed, a job that almost never ceases: the dissemination of mail, newsletters, and other miscellaneous missives to the all-important (even to the majority leader) Folks

178

Back Home. Senators cater to their constituents in this way both from their offices in Washington and from their home states. In Washington, Baker receives between 4,000 and 5,000 letters a week from constituents, and gone are the days when, as one Baker staffer recalls it, all or most of them were tossed into the trash. Senators have to be public relations minded now, and treat their offices like small businesses.

Baker has an entire operation in the Hart building devoted to keeping the constituency happy. They spend most of their time answering constituent mail and working with Baker's Tennessee offices. The elaborate IBM "System 6" has been programmed to sign Baker's signature with an automatic pen. Letters written by legislative correspondents and approved by Baker's administration assistant David Spear are then personalized by a machine—signed, sealed, and all but delivered. The typical reply nimbly avoids controversy, no matter what the subject of the letter, and eschews dogmatic stands on current issues. That kind of artful dodging has become more necessary since Baker became majority leader, because often he winds up voting the way he does for reasons of procedural expediency or commitments made to committee chairmen who want matters expedited. Voting one's conscience on some great moral matter is a thrill that senators experience rarely, if ever.

All the addresses of those who write to Baker are kept on file; they will be put on the senator's Christmas list; everybody who writes gets holiday greetings from Senator Baker each December. It was and is common Senate practice.

For all Baker knows, his IBM System 6 may be sending out IOUs or proposals of marriage; he only drops by the Hart building offices about once a year to visit his mail-inundated staff. In a sense, this is fine with the staff members: they don't have to worry about the senator storming out of his office or summoning them abruptly. But this ultraautonomy does give them a sense of isolation, of being on the distant periphery of the action. From their point of view, virtually every other Senate office has an air of excitement to it, in the sense that the office will get caught up on any given day in what the boss is doing, what kind of mood he is in, how blow the political winds, even if they themselves have no voice in the substantive matters. Most of the Baker staff members who work in the Hart building have never even met him.

They feel cheated, distanced, even exiled. They want to get to know the old boy, even though they are told by those who work closely with him that you can spend every day working at his side and still feel you haven't gotten to know him. He is considered warm and fair, but not expansive and certainly not gregarious. There are many names and faces of individuals working for him at Hart that Baker does not know. If by chance they visit the Capitol and say hello to him in the hallway, Baker will be able to greet them only with an embarrassed look on his face.

If the staffers in Hart feel distanced, the Baker staff in Tennessee feel downright forgotten, as if they are drifting about in a space station a few million miles from earth. Some may feel they are employed by The Wizard of Oz—that man behind the curtain whom they know mainly as an apparition on a television screen whenever Baker makes news. Baker doesn't travel back to Tennessee as much as other members travel to their home states. Most members, even those from the West, try to make a trip home at least twice a month; many in fact now make the trip weekly. But Baker can't spare the time for these trips. He has to go around the country stumping for other Republicans, and when that duty doesn't call, he likes puttering in the darkroom or the greenhouse of his Washington home.

To help Baker take care of constituents, he, like all senators, has staff and offices in other cities—in Memphis, Knoxville, Nashville, and Chattanooga, plus an office of sorts in the Tri-Cities, where a woman works out of her home, and a private secretary in his hometown of Huntsville. That state operation has not enjoyed the best of reputations in the past; when William Brock was still in the Senate, it was said that Brock survived because of his staff, and Baker survived in spite of his staff.

For Baker's Tennessee staff, his trips back to the state are an example of just how much he gets away with because of his own personal affability. Disgruntled constituent groups will insist on seeing Baker personally during his next trip home. Baker's Tennessee staff will agonize over the upcoming meetings because they fear they might be among the constituent grievances Baker will hear about. They would discuss canceling the meetings, but they know Baker would tell them no, no, don't cancel; he'll handle the group when he gets there. No matter how overtly displeased members of these groups are before their meetings with Baker, they always walk out of them smiling like the winners of beauty pageants. He does it with charm and charisma and Senate star quality. Much of Baker's success and popularity as a senator has nothing to do with legislative or administrative brilliance. It has to do with being a great juggler and a Dr. Feelgood besides. Howard Baker knows how to leave 'em smiling when he says adieu. Some are not just smiling, they're dazzled.

Unfortunately, by the time of Baker's next trip home, new groups will have been angered, or previously placated groups will manage to get grumpy all over again. And so it will go.

Baker has never really had a typical sort of constituent operation. Newsletters are the preferred public relations medium for many members, but Baker's office is certainly not in the running for newsletter-of-the-year honors. James Sasser, the other Tennessee senator, had more than 600,000 Tennessee names on the mailing lists for his newsletters; Baker has about 50,000. During this April, senators will have sent out some 16.5 million newsletters, in addition to more than 1 million "town meeting" mailings, which offer yet another excuse to write home.

At 12:35 P.M., Air Force One is "wheels up" from Andrews, and Baker and Reagan are en route to Houston. Baker's press secretary Tommy Griscom is in the backup plane. Baker and Reagan touch down in Houston at 2:25. At that moment, William Cohen of Maine is still up in the air, in more ways than one. Cohen is on another plane flying to the Tower fundraiser; he has been quoted in this morning's *New York Times* making what sounds like an anti-Tower remark. He is acutely embarrassed, and angry, about the whole thing. Like innumerable politicians before him and countless to come after, Cohen is insisting that he has been quoted out of context. When reporter Steve Roberts had asked Cohen if he thought that Tower was out of step with the times, Cohen responded, "He's been saying the same thing for 20 years." The paper didn't report or perceive that Cohen meant that as a compliment, a reference to Tower's dogged consistency. Cohen has heard that Tower is angry about the remark, too; the quotation does seem harmonious with common criticisms of Tower—that he is a reactionary, that he is one of the great legislators of the nineteenth century, and so on. In the Senate, it is considered bad form to criticize a colleague publicly, and especially bad form for the member of a committee, in this case the armed services committee, to take a poke at the chairman in print. Cohen, widely regarded as one of the most intelligent men in the Senate, is so chagrined that he is making plans to point a finger at the *Times* on the Senate floor when Monday rolls around. Senators' feelings can bruise as easily as those of Hollywood starlets.

Back in Washington, there is *some* serious business being done on this largely frivolous Friday. The Senate rarely looks at large issues, because it is so preoccupied with day-to-day events. But this afternoon, staffs of two of the Senate's best big thinkers are at work on a comprehensive nuclear build-down plan. In the Hart building, Senator Cohen's assistant, Bob Savitt, is looking over a letter to President Reagan outlining their proposal for nuclear build-down. When Savitt is finished, the letter will be delivered to the staff of Senator Sam Nunn (D–Ga.) for further work.

When an issue as complicated as nuclear build-down comes along, senators depend even more extensively on the expertise of their staffs than they usually do. Nunn and Cohen are probably the reigning experts in the Senate on the subject, but Cohen is relying heavily on Savitt nevertheless. Savitt has a Ph.D. in strategic studies from Georgetown University. He started work in January 1983 on a fellowship from the State Department, where he dealt with arms control and intelligence work, after working at the Department of Defense for six years.

The most important thing that Cohen and Nunn have going for them is their credibility on the issue. Senators recognize leaders in many areas, and these two wield a great amount of power because of their reputations. Cohen and Nunn are both known as individuals who do their homework and keep things in perspective.

Lautenberg has left Washington for the week; he is off on another of his many television station tours of the home state. At one station he tapes an edition of something called "New Jersey Perspectives."

Back in Washington, his staff is hard at work. Checchi is leading a meeting of the legislative team on the budget issues that will be coming up the following week. She will again brief the senator on budget matters when he returns to Washington after the weekend at his home in Montclair.

Checchi is too busy to give much more than fleeting thought to her imminent retirement from Lautenberg's staff; still, it does cross her mind. Things are settling down now. Lautenberg's remedial education is almost complete, and she is beginning to feel like the Lone Ranger nearing the end of a good deed. Then, too, she doesn't have to feel in any way disloyal for leaving Lautenberg's staff at this point, because the staff entrance has been a revolving door ever since Lautenberg threw his expensive hat into the ring and began his race.

Frank Lautenberg's election to the Senate in 1982 was a monumental victory. He won for two main reasons: television and money. The odds had been overwhelmingly against him but, in the modern era of Senate campaigning, enough TV and enough money can have the effect of evening out the odds. Lautenberg had never run for public office at any level before. His recognition factor in the state at the time of his decision to run was hovering around the 4 percent mark. Worse yet, after being successful enough to win the Democratic nomination, he found himself challenging a certified political legend, one of the more popular political figures in the country; Millicent Fenwick, crusty pipe-smoking granny, 20-year Hill veteran, and darling of the media.

Those close to Lautenberg weren't surprised by his decision to run. They knew him as a self-made multimillionaire, chief executive officer of Automatic Data Processing, the company he cofounded, and without question his own boss; they also knew he had been a political dabbler for years. He was attracted to power—the old story—and because in an ingenuous sort of way Lautenberg held on to the belief that individuals make a difference and there was a lot that he wanted to do to help others. His Democratic roots were fairly deep. In 1972, he handed George McGovern $90,000 of his own money for McGovern's ill-fated presidential adventure and held McGovern fundraisers at his lavish Montclair home. Isaac Stern entertained the guests at one, and Arthur Ashe and George Plimpton played tennis, on Lautenberg's private courts, at another.

When Harrison Williams' Abscam troubles got too big to ignore, Lautenberg's ambitious wheels started turning. It became achingly clear that Williams, who had been in the Senate since 1956, would not be running again, and the time looked emphatically right for Lautenberg to make his move.

One of the first exploratory trips Lautenberg made was to New York to seek the advice of political guru David Garth. He told Garth about his desire to run. Garth told him to forget it. It wasn't because Lautenberg was inexperienced or because Fenwick was a political Graf Spee, Garth said, but because Garth was convinced Lautenberg's campaign would unearth what he considered to be latent anti-Semitism in the state of New Jersey, crippling Lautenberg's candidacy. Lautenberg actually took what Garth said as encouraging; he didn't think that being Jewish was any barrier, and if that was what Garth considered to be the main obstacle, there was hope.

So Lautenberg threw himself body and soul into a ten-candidate race. At first it was more soul than body, because there was a part of Lautenberg that didn't want to leave his job at ADP; he hoped instead that the voters would come beseechingly to him. He didn't have a realistic understanding of the sacrifices involved, or of the way his life would be turned inside out, but fortunately he eventually gathered around him a staff that did understand; he supplemented his kitchen cabinet with emigrés from the outgoing Brendan Byrne administration. Joe Grandmaison, a hard-shelled veteran of many a campaign, was hired as campaign manager, and despite his bossy, abrasive style—one that would lead to numerous shouting matches with Lautenberg—Grandmaison was, in the opinion of many of those close to Lautenberg, just what was needed.

Grandmaison knew that Lautenberg's low recognition was the first problem to deal with if he was going to survive the primary. He realized he had to make Lautenberg understand, first, the severe time constraints he was under and, second, that he was merely the candidate—he couldn't give all the orders any more because he wouldn't know the right orders to give. Lautenberg was a natural at talking to crowds and shaking hands and pushing himself into photogenic situations, but a self-made man finds nothing natural about taking orders from advisors. It requires massive readjustment. A man or woman running for the Senate for the first time, seeking an office imagined to wield enormous power, can start out with a feeling of powerlessness that is in some way prophetic of things to come, should the campaign prove successful.

Lautenberg overcame his chronic unrecognizability with a large transfusion of funds—$1 million from his own pocket for the primary campaign—and won the nomination. He was the only one of the ten candidates in the field to make extensive use of paid television time, and it would serve him well in the general election to come.

The general election campaign was more difficult than the

primary, not only because of the enormity of challenging Fenwick-the-seemingly-invincible, but also because the Lautenberg game plan was the kind whose effectiveness wouldn't be known until the campaign's end, when it would be a bit too late to change strategies.

For his campaign staff, the first task was to make Lautenberg better known; the second was to convince voters he would be not only good for New Jersey, but better for New Jersey than Fenwick; the third was to try to set the tone of the campaign, by hammering away on those issues that would benefit Lautenberg; and the fourth was to attack Fenwick's national-senator reputation and the way she had flip-flopped on issues over the years. Pollster Peter D. Hart stressed repeatedly to Lautenberg, however, that Mrs. Fenwick was never to be attacked personally. "Under no circumstances should there be any personal criticism of her," he wrote in August as part of an 11-page campaign memo.

Fenwick's campaign people, meanwhile, were not impressed with the newcomer to politics, nor where they at all worried. In fact, they were practically dividing up the jobs they wanted when they all got down to merry old Washington. Fenwick's failure to take Lautenberg's campaign seriously, and to deal with Lautenberg seriously as a challenger, was, beyond television and money, a key factor in Lautenberg's victory. Fenwick was also a victim of anti-Reagan sentiment then growing in the state. She had allied herself closely with Reagan to defeat Jeffrey Bell, a young and articulate conservative during the primary, and now was stuck with her Reagan ties as New Jerseyans grew increasingly unhappy over high unemployment and Reaganomics.

In his August memo, pollster Hart listed the three elements Lautenberg should stress in his campaign: his Horatio Alger background and its contrast to Mrs. Fenwick's genteel image ("Show that you know and understand what kind of struggle the average person is going through because for more than half your life, you faced that same struggle to put food on the table and try to get ahead"); his concept of a senator's duty ("It is crucial to portray yourself as a senator who sees his first priority as fighting for New Jersey"); and his business credentials and commitment to economic development, and thus more jobs, for the state ("He must make this the single most important and, indeed, the only issue in this campaign").

Hart ended his memo by telling Lautenberg, "At present, Millicent Fenwick leads by a decisive 53 percent to 25 percent margin, but we have all seen many contests in which the underdog has triumphed. You too can beat the odds, but success will require a tremendous amount of discipline and a lot of money. . . . Good luck, my friend."

Lautenberg largely stuck with the Hart plan. But he did not stick with Hart. As the campaign wore on, he grew uneasy with him and decided to hire another pollster, though Hart did stay on in an advisory capacity. Bob Squires was brought in to replace David Sawyer as director of the television campaign. Lautenberg felt that Sawyer was up to the primary race but not up to the fight against Fenwick, and he knew how important a weapon television was in that fight. More dramatically, the shouting matches between Lautenberg and Grandmaison were increasing in frequency and intensity. Grandmaison, whose bare-knuckle approach had been so necessary in the early stages of the campaign, became an emotional burden that an increasingly war-weary Lautenberg would no longer endure. He fired Grandmaison and replaced him with Tim Ridley.

Squire's company, Communications Inc., has an in-house production unit that makes commercials; it thus exercises complete control on behalf of the candidates it represents. The contract Lautenberg signed entitled Squires to $50,000 plus 15 percent of "the buy"—the buy being the total amount spent on radio and television time. That buy grew into an enormous sum; since New Jersey has no major television station to call its own, it is not so much a market as a zone between two of the nation's biggest: New York and Philadelphia, respectively, the number one and four markets in the country. Stations in the two cities command premium rates, and Lautenberg had to pay them.

The three main areas for the commercials were, first, the big issue, jobs; second, the candidates' orientations—Lautenberg devoted to New Jersey, Fenwick more of a national or even international politician; and, third, the Fenwick inconsistency, which the Lautenbergers dubbed "flip-flop."

The careful, nonpersonal attacks on Fenwick started to work, and Fenwick became noticeably testy. In one debate, she tried to make an issue of Lautenberg's wealth, saying that at least she didn't "drive around town in a Mercedes." Lautenberg was then asked if it was true he drove around in a Mercedes, and Lautenberg, the owner of a Porsche 911 Targa valued at more than $40,000, said no, he didn't own one.

In the first week of October, the unemployment statistics came out and put the national unemployment rate at 10.1 percent; it was good news for Lautenberg. With jobs a key issue and his TV-transmitted charisma a key asset, he scored his upset victory.

It is 6:30 on a Houston evening, and Howard Baker has just arrived at the Thomas Convention Center for the "general reception," another leg in the long fundraising journey. He has already been to a VIP reception for the really big donors. It strikes him that this is one of the biggest fundraising events he has ever attended. The planning for it has been going on for nine months. Tower's people wanted to give the impression that he is an incumbent of considerable power and clout, and to do that it is necessary for them to secure a presidential appearance, which they have done. It doesn't hurt to have Baker there bestowing his presence on the occasion, either; and though Baker is far more moderate politically than Tower, he is glad to make the trip.

Tower asked Brad O'Leary, head of Political Affairs Management, a Washington-based firm that arranges such events, to handle the plans for the fundraiser. PAM only does dinners designed to raise $400,000 or more, and only for Republicans. For tonight's affair they are charging Tower $25,000, and it's worth it. The original plan for this one was to raise $750,000, but it wound up bringing in $1.5 million. Tickets were priced from $200 to $1,000 each.

Naturally, in such a massive operation, there are bound to be logistical difficulties. When one has 14 Republican senators present, they all have to be given roles to play, functions to fill. Stevens and Percy, for instance, were assigned to press flesh at a cocktail reception. There would be breakfasts and two luncheons as well. At a cocktail party for 1,100, guests are asked to wear nametags so they can be easily identified by photographers from local newspapers and TV stations. The nametags are color-coded to facilitate distinguishing big shots from small.

And then there arises the kind of problem that couldn't very well have been foreseen: James A. Baker, White House chief of staff, decides in the midst of one of the parties that, gee, a beer would taste good right now. A beer? Mr. Baker wants a beer! And nary a beer in the place. So, embarrassed Tower aides dispatch another Tower aide to a nearby 7-Eleven to buy beer—except there is no store nearby, and it takes several minutes before a six-pack is ceremoniously produced.

Howard Baker gives a short speech praising Tower and his contributions to the Senate and emphasizing the importance of keeping the Republican majority. Tower is worried. Since his first election to the Senate, in a special contest to replace newly elected Vice President Lyndon B. Johnson, in 1961, his victories have all been squeakers. The money tonight is to help him do battle with what would surely be tough and determined competition through the '84 election. Ronald Reagan's bravado invigorates him. In his speech, Reagan ridicules the way the Carter administration handled economic ills. "You remember, they called it a malaise," says Reagan. "And now former Vice President Malaise is running for president, promising he can do everything just like they did before."

His fundraising, handshaking, and backslapping chores complete, Howard Baker flies back to Washington, and to Joy, the next morning on a private plane he uses for such getaways. The week's wrangles over immigration, Central America, and the budget are behind him and, for the moment, forgotten. They will be back in his head on Monday morning; this he knows. On Air Force One, Reagan gives reporters an earful: that were he to seek a second term, he would want George Bush on the ticket with him again, because "you don't break up a combination that's working," although he is leaving open the possibility Bush might decline to serve another four years. Reagan says, "I understand when there comes a time when someone says, 'Enough already.' "

Five months later John Tower says, "Enough already." He decides to retire from the Senate and not seek reelection. All that money so elaborately raised in Houston is channeled to another deserving Republican. Even John Tower, who's been known for his lust for the battle, has raised the white flag and left the field.

While in Houston, Simpson finds himself surrounded by many who really don't approve of his immigration bill. He knows that the proximity of the Mexican border heightened awareness of the problems of immigration; many at the party tonight would have preferred the legislation to be tougher on alien entry.

But their preferences will eventually prove to be meaningless. The immigration bill does not exactly face clear sailing ahead.

In three weeks, Simpson returns to the Senate floor with his immigration proposal. He fights hard, beating back all amendments from both sides that threaten its survival, winning on the ones he has to. On May 6, he stands in the well and watches the Senate overwhelmingly pass his bill.

But the year and the battle are not over. He spends months keeping his eye on what the House does with the measure. When it finally passes an immigration bill of its own, he drags his prized staffer Richard Day along through an arduous, month-long conference process. It is painstaking. It is exhaustive. Memos fill desks. And then, in the end, all for nothing. The conference fails to come up with a compromise plan. The legislation is dead.

Simpson remains sanguine. He does have the consolations of philosophy. "When you lose, take a deep gulp, and put a smile on your face, and get on to the next son-of-a-bitch item of business," he says. "Instead of just trying every single whiz-bang trick, post-cloture, over-the-head cloture, twist-em-tail cloture—you name it—you know, someday, you've got to end it. You can't seek perfection in legislation. You don't have it in life, so how the hell can you look for it in legislation?"

He regards the legislative process with pragmatic realism. "I don't think of it as high drama, because if you do your homework and you're fully prepared and you have a good staff, you can get something passed," he says, but he also adds, "Everything you do in legislating hangs by a thread. You can pass something in one body by a vote of 100 to nothing and say, 'Wow, wasn't that something!' And then go over to the other body and get beat, 320 to 10, you know. That's the way it works, so you don't have time to savor a victory or indulge yourself in defeat, or pity yourself, which is a pretty good way to have it progress. To put it on the basis of win or lose, no. I'm not joyous when I win or downhearted when I lose. I'm like—there's an old Rudyard Kipling quote: 'If you can meet with triumph and disaster and treat those two imposters as the same.' "

The fate of Chris Dodd's Central America mission isn't so cut-and-dried as the disposition of Simpson's immigration bill. The issue will be around for years to come. It is chewed up a thousand times in the Senate—by committees, in caucuses, on the floor—and then by the House. Dodd begins to view it as a lifelong struggle.

Dodd, however, does not subscribe to the popular philosophy that such problems as Central America would have been more handily and efficaciously dealt with by senates of the past. He is determinedly optimistic about the Senate of the present. "I don't place a great deal of stock in the lament of the more senior members about what the institution looks like today vis à vis what it looked like 20 or 15 or 35 years ago," says this senator's son. "I think any time you come to the United States Senate is an opportune time. It's such a tremendous forum, a place where you really can accomplish things. It's much harder in the House to have an impact. In the Senate, there's a far greater opportunity to have an impact. So I don't place a great deal of emphasis on this notion that it was better 20 years ago, or it's better today. We're here, and we've got the membership to deal with, and all the problems. To waste a lot of time wishing it were like 1912 or 1935 or 1960 or something is interesting cloakroom conversation, but it doesn't mean a whole lot to me."

Steve Bell's work on the budget continues, though not always according to schedule. The budget does come to a vote the next week but, after a week of haggling, Bell fails in his efforts to get Domenici to go along with the Democrats for the sake of a budget—any budget—and the Senate winds up voting to submit the bill to the budget committee once again. Bell has to go through the entire committee episode once more, only to learn that there are no new compromises and ultimately no clear way out. When the budget finally does arrive back on the Senate floor, during the first week of May, it faces a Republican–Democrat standoff. Neither side can assume victory. Howard Baker is quoted as looking on the positive side of the impasse: "I don't have 50 votes," he said, "but they don't have 50 votes either." One week later the budget passes by one vote—Howard Baker's.

Within a month of Mary Jane Checchi's second thoughts about remaining on the Hill, she is gone again. This time she vows never to return, knowing full well it is a vow that may be broken. Having been exposed to the innermost workings of the Senate, she still feels that the challenges outside the chamber appeal to her more.

Howard Baker's days in the Senate are numbered, too. His plans to seek the presidential nomination in 1988 grow firmer when Reagan declares he's running for reelection in 1984. But Baker, still wincing from the unhappy experience of running for president while simultaneously serving in the senate in 1980, looks forward to life without the Senate. He returns to the law when his term in the Senate ends, serving one law firm in Washington and one in Tennessee. And he joins the board of directors of no less than four major corporations.

His appetite for politics seems undiminished, even if his appetite for the Senate is sated. Before he leaves, he insists he cares little about how historians will treat his years as majority leader. "I have no idea," he says. "I don't even think about it. I always believe and continue to believe, although I know deep down it's probably not true, at least not altogether true, that the minute I leave the Senate, my experience here will evaporate. That it'll just disappear. It's sort of a protective mechanism, because it keeps me from worrying about what people will think or what the future may hold. Deep down inside of me, there's something that says, you know, that I'm writing with disappearing ink. That I just do what I do and I do the best I can and not worry about it."

He does not leave, however, with no worries about the Senate itself. "The strength of the Senate most recently—meaning since World War II—has, in my opinion, come from that middle ground, that is, people who are not very wealthy, but who have an abiding concern about public affairs. And if you're in public affairs, there's almost no opportunity to accumulate wealth. But that group, unless we do something about it, is going to get pushed out of politics and certainly pushed out of the Senate. We're going to be left with people who have personal resources, and they usually are going to be older rather than younger, or people who are very young and think there's still time to accumulate wealth afterward. Or who don't care. But the way the pay thing operates now, it's going to change the character and the function of the Senate over the years and it's not going to change it for the better."

By leaving the Senate, Howard Baker increases his annual salary from $75,000 to approximately $1 million.

On November 16, 1984, Baker says his official farewells. On the Senate floor, he is rousingly praised and cheered by his colleagues. He will be succeeded as majority leader by Bob Dole of Kansas. Dole announces early that he has no intention of pursuing Howard Baker's long, fruitless battle to open the Senate chamber to television cameras. The idea appears to be dead.

Jim Range, the legislative cowboy, leaves Baker's office in the spring of 1984. He takes a job as vice president at a firm called Waste Management Inc. From that position, he will often return to the Hill—as a lobbyist. And in doing so, he will double his annual income.

Just before he leaves, Range can be found spending a lot of time across the hall from Baker's Capitol Hill office, in the suite of offices occupied by Senator Ted Stevens. Range is not there for love of Senator Stevens. He had lived with another Senate staffer for four years, then broken up with her; now he is dating Stevens' chief of staff, Rebecca Gernhart.

On September 4, 1984, they are married in a private ceremony at a small church in Leesburg, Virginia.

Index

Budget and Accounting Act, 38–39
budget committee, 38–48
  Bell as staff director of, 16, 38, 40, 44, 58, 72–73, 99–100, 109, 116, 168, 192
  Domenici as chairman of, 38, 40, 41, 44–47, 48, 71–72, 79, 80, 83–84, 87, 116, 141
Bumpers, Dale, 59
Bundy, McGeorge, 66
Burford, Ann, 169, 170
Bush, George, 80, 88, 190
Byrd, Robert:
  Baker's relationship with, 29, 32–33, 50, 98, 108, 109
  daily routine of, 21
  Dodd and, 107–8
  as minority leader, 50, 57, 84–85, 101, 139, 141, 142, 163, 166
  personality of, 85
  staff of, 60
Byrne, Brendan, 185

Caddell, Patrick, 106, 129
Cannon, James, 30, 33, 74, 79, 80, 144, 169
Capitol, U.S.:
  damage to West Front of, 132, 134–35, 136–37
  preservation and renovation of, 25–26, 132, 134–35, 136–38, 173–74
  rotunda of, 96–97
Capitol Hill Club, 66–68
Capitol Page School, 49
Carey, Freeman, 25, 178
Carter, Jimmy, 69, 147, 189
CBS News, 124–25, 126–27
Central America:
  closed Senate session on, 16, 22, 32–33, 50, 55, 56–57, 80, 84, 87, 88, 89, 90–94, 105, 191–92
  misrepresentation of issues about, 107
  Soviet influence in, 130

U.S. policy toward, 16, 22, 33, 50, 56, 68, 88–89, 90–94, 97, 98, 100, 106, 107, 124–31, 142, 191–92
Chafee, John, 89, 172–73
Checchi, Mary Jane, 156
  as aide to Byrd, 85
  as aide to Lautenberg, 16, 54, 55, 60, 61–63, 64, 93, 109, 112, 113, 114–15, 138–39, 157
  writing career of, 60–61, 168, 183, 192–93
Chiles, Lawton, 42, 43, 46–47, 85–86, 164, 166
Citadel (White), 28
Civil Rights Act (1964), 104
civil rights movement, 104, 146
classified documents, 91, 93, 94
Cleveland Jewish Federation, 55
cloture motion, 101, 161–62
Cohen, Kevin, 175
Cohen, William, 89, 175, 181–83
commerce committee, 54, 55, 64, 94
committees:
  hearings of, 35–36, 62, 63, 65, 137–38
  standing, 80
  testimony before, 62
  weekly meetings for chairmen of, 80–84
  see also specific committees
Communications Inc., 187
concurrent resolutions, 39
Congress, U.S.:
  fiscal policies of, 39
  joint sessions of, 22, 33, 89, 90, 97, 100, 121, 124–31, 142
  as network of fiefdoms, 105
  original theory vs. contemporary practice of, 9–13
  power structure of, 70, 103, 173, 184, 185
  reorganization of, 104–5
  unequal employment practices of, 103–4

immigration subcommittee,
37–38, 80, 81–83, 120, 141,
145, 147–53, 163–64, 165,
166, 190–91
"imperial presidency," 68–69
intelligence committee, 33, 87,
88, 91–92
Israel, U.S. aid to, 145

Jackson, Henry, 109
Jefferson, Thomas, 157–58
Jepsen, Roger, 79, 98
John Paul II, Pope, 128
Johnson, Lyndon B., 69–70, 146,
189

Kassebaum, Nancy, 88, 103,
130–31
Kennedy, Edward M., 53, 101,
106, 120, 152
as member of immigration subcommittee, 147, 150,
163–64, 165
Kennedy, John F., 20, 26, 70,
120, 146
Kipling, Rudyard, 191

labor and human resources committee, 65
Lautenberg, Frank R.:
Checchi as aide to, 16, 54, 55,
60, 61–63, 64, 93, 109, 112,
113, 114–15, 138–39, 157
closed session missed by,
93–94, 105
election campaign of, 112,
113–14, 183–88
as former businessman, 63, 113,
115, 139–40, 188
as freshman senator, 16, 54–55,
114–15, 139–40, 164
as member of banking committee, 62–65, 109
as member of commerce committee, 94
New Jersey constituency of,
64–65
staff of, 54, 93–94, 112–13

Laxalt, Paul, 80, 151
Baker and, 53–54
as friend of Reagan, 41, 68, 95
Leahy, Patrick, 131
Lebatore, Rob, 57, 107, 130
legislation:
amendments to, 35–36, 37
debate on, 36, 38, 48, 65, 141
floor consideration of, 36, 37,
48, 65, 147
flow of, 35–37
hearings on, 35–36, 62,
137–138
"held at the desk," 147
"mark-up" of, 35–36, 42, 100
pending, 31, 36
"reporting out" of, 36, 40, 47,
66, 119
scheduling of, 24
strategy for, 31, 59
legislative branch appropriations
subcommittee, 132, 135–36,
137
legislative correspondents, 110, 179
legislative directors, 110
Legislative Reorganization Acts
(1946 and 1970), 104–5
letters, constituent, 111–12, 114
Levin, Carl, 109
Library of Congress, 25, 135
Liebengood, Howard, 90
lobbyists, 61–62, 147–49, 155–56,
194
Long, Russell, 123
Lott, Trent, 68
Lubalin, Eve, 61, 113, 157
Luger, Richard, 53, 54, 89

McAdams, Mike, 129
McCarthy, Eugene, 73
McClure, James, 53, 66, 81, 87,
115, 116
McGovern, George, 184
Mansfield, Mike, 70, 85
Marshall, George, 12
Massey, Don, 138
Mathias, Charles, 135, 139, 147,
165
Matsunaga, Spark, 154

About the Author

James A. Miller was a member of the Television Reporting Team at *The Washington Post* before becoming special assistant and chief speechwriter to Senate majority leader Howard Baker in 1981. He grew up in Bucks County, Pennsylvania, and received his A.B. degree from Occidental College in California and an M. Litt. degree from Oxford University, England. His articles have appeared in *The New York Times*, *Newsweek*, *Life* and *The Harvard Journal on Legislation*. Miller is currently a producer at CBS news.

```
JK      Miller,  James A.
1161     (James  Andrew),
M55      1957-
1987
C.1     Running  in place
```

DATE			